NELSON GOODMAN

LANGUAGES

OF ART

AN APPROACH
TO A THEORY OF SYMBOLS

LONDON
OXFORD UNIVERSITY PRESS
1969

Oxford University Press, Ely House, London W. 1

GLASGOW MELBOURNE WELLINGTON

CAPE TOWN SALISBURY IBADAN NAIROBI LUSAKA ADDIS ABABA

BOMBAY CALCUTTA MADRAS KARACHI LAHORE DACCA

KUALA LUMPUR SINGAPORE HONG KONG TOKYO

Library of Congress Catalog Card Number 68-31825

REPRINTED LITHOGRAPHICALLY IN GREAT BRITAIN
BY COMPTON PRINTING LTD., LONDON AND AYLESBURY

LANGUAGES OF ART

OTHER BOOKS BY NELSON GOODMAN

The Structure of Appearance

Fact, Fiction, and Forecast

PREFACE

The lines of thought that joined my interest in the arts with my inquiries into the theory of knowledge began to emerge some ten years ago. An invitation a couple of years later to give the John Locke Lectures at Oxford in 1962 led to the organization of accumulated material into six lectures. These formed the basis for the present much revised and expanded chapters.

My indebtedness to institutions and individuals is uncomfortably high in relation to the results. A year at the Center for Cognitive Studies at Harvard University and subsequent support by the National Science Foundation (under grant GS 978) and the Old Dominion Foundation made possible a wider and more detailed investigation than could otherwise have been undertaken. As a philosopher squarely in the Socratic tradition of knowing nothing, I have depended upon experts and practitioners in fields where my study has had to intrude. Among these are:—in psychology, Paul A. Kolers; in linguistics, S. Jay Keyser; in the visual arts, Meyer Schapiro and Katharine Sturgis; in music, George Rochberg, Harold Shapero, and Joyce Mekeel; in dance and dance notation, Ina Hahn, Anne Hutchinson Guest, and Lucy Venable.

I have also profited from discussions with my graduate students and with philosophers and others at the University of Pennsylvania, Oxford, Harvard, Princeton, Cornell, and other universities where versions of some of these chapters have been given as lectures. Finally, such virtues and faults

PREFACE

as the book may have are in part due to the help of my research assistants, especially Robert Schwartz, Marsha Hanen, and Hoyt Hobbs. Much of the proofreading and the indexing has been done by Lynn Foster and Geoffrey Hellman.

Harvard University

CONTENTS

CONTENTS

CONTENTS

V
SCORE, SKETCH, AND SCRIPT

VI
ART AND THE UNDERSTANDING

INTRODUCTION

Though this book deals with some problems pertaining to the arts, its scope does not coincide very closely with what is ordinarily taken to be the field of aesthetics. On the one hand, I touch only incidentally on questions of value, and offer no canons of criticism. No mandatory judgments are implied concerning any work I cite as an example, and the reader is invited to substitute his own illustrations. On the other hand, my study ranges beyond the arts into matters pertaining to the sciences, technology, perception, and practice. Problems concerning the arts are points of departure rather than of convergence. The objective is an approach to a general theory of symbols.

"Symbol" is used here as a very general and colorless term. It covers letters, words, texts, pictures, diagrams, maps, models, and more, but carries no implication of the oblique or the occult. The most literal portrait and the most prosaic passage are as much symbols, and as 'highly symbolic', as the most fanciful and figurative.

Systematic inquiry into the varieties and functions of symbols has seldom been undertaken. Expanding investigation in structural linguistics in recent years needs to be supplemented by and integrated with intensive examination of nonverbal symbol systems, from pictorial representation on the one hand to musical notation on the other, if we are to achieve any comprehensive grasp of the modes and means of reference and of their varied and pervasive use in the operations of the understanding. "Languages" in my title should, strictly, be replaced by "symbol systems". But the title, since always read before the book, has been kept in the vernacular. The nonreader will not mind, and the reader will understand—as the reader of my first book understands that the more accurate title would be "Structures of Appearance".

The six chapters, from their titles and their origin in lectures, might seem to be a collection of essays on loosely related topics. Actually, the structure of the book is rather intricate; two routes of investigation, one beginning in the first chapter and the other in the third, merge only in the last. No such simple warning, however, will overcome another difficulty some readers may face: while a layman should have little trouble with most of the book, he will encounter terms, paragraphs, and sections that assume some background in technical philosophy; and much of Chapter IV will be hard going for any stranger to elementary logic. Nevertheless, by reading around the technical passages, almost anyone can gather enough of what is under way to decide whether to make the effort needed to understand what he has skipped.

Layman or not, the reader must be prepared to find his convictions and his common sense—that repository of ancient error—often outraged by what he finds here. I have repeatedly had to assail authoritative current doctrine and fond prevailing faith. Yet I claim no outstanding novelty for my conclusions. I am by no means unaware of contributions to symbol theory by such philosophers as Peirce, Cassirer, Morris, and Langer; and while I reject one after another of the views common to much of the literature of aesthetics, most of my arguments and results may well have been anticipated by other writers. Yet since any attempt to trace the complex pattern of my agreement and disagreement with each or even any of these writers would give a purely historical matter disproportionate and distracting prominence, I can only make this blanket apology to those who may in effect already have written what they read here. However, where I have consulted specific works by psychologists and by writers on the several arts, I have tried always to give detailed references.

Frequently some result of my own earlier philosophical work has been brought to bear here, but I have tried not to regrind old axes. For instance, if some of the following pages violate the principles of nominalism, that is only because it seems unnecessary for me to show, for present purposes, how a nominalistic version may be formulated.

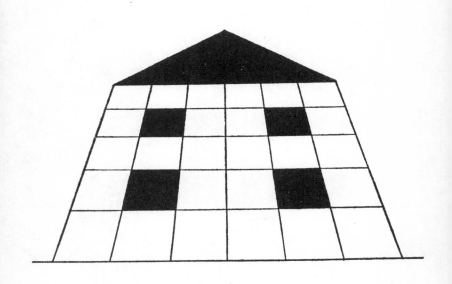

Reverse

Drawing from Paul Klee's *Pädagogische Skizzenbuch* (Munich, 1925; 2nd American edition, New York, Frederick A. Praeger, Inc., 1953), p. 41; reproduced here by permission of the publishers.

I

REALITY REMADE

Art is not a copy of the real world. One of the damn things is enough. *

1. Denotation

Whether a picture ought to be a representation or not is a question much less crucial than might appear from current bitter battles among artists, critics, and propagandists. Nevertheless, the nature of representation wants early study in any philosophical examination of the ways symbols function in and out of the arts. That representation is frequent in some arts, such as painting, and infrequent in others, such as music, threatens trouble for a unified aesthetics; and confusion over how pictorial representation as a mode of signification is allied to and distinguished from verbal description on the one hand and, say, facial expression on the other is fatal to any general theory of symbols.

The most naive view of representation might perhaps be put somewhat like this: "*A* represents *B* if and only if *A* appreciably resembles *B*", or "*A* represents *B* to the extent that *A* resembles *B*". Vestiges of this view, with assorted refinements, persist in most writing on representation. Yet

* Reported as occurring in an essay on Virginia Woolf. I have been unable to locate the source.

more error could hardly be compressed into so short a formula.

Some of the faults are obvious enough. An object resembles itself to the maximum degree but rarely represents itself; resemblance, unlike representation, is reflexive. Again, unlike representation, resemblance is symmetric: B is as much like A as A is like B, but while a painting may represent the Duke of Wellington, the Duke doesn't represent the painting. Furthermore, in many cases neither one of a pair of very like objects represents the other: none of the automobiles off an assembly line is a picture of any of the rest; and a man is not normally a representation of another man, even his twin brother. Plainly, resemblance in any degree is no sufficient condition for representation.[1]

Just what correction to make in the formula is not so obvious. We may attempt less, and prefix the condition "If A is a picture, . . .". Of course, if we then construe "picture" as "representation", we resign a large part of the question: namely, what constitutes a representation. But

[1] What I am considering here is pictorial representation, or depiction, and the comparable representation that may occur in other arts. Natural objects may represent in the same way: witness the man in the moon and the sheep-dog in the clouds. Some writers use "representation" as the general term for all varieties of what I call symbolization or reference, and use "symbolic" for the verbal and other nonpictorial signs I call nonrepresentational. "Represent" and its derivatives have many other uses, and while I shall mention some of these later, others do not concern us here at all. Among the latter, for example, are the uses according to which an ambassador represents a nation and makes representations to a foreign government.

even if we construe "picture" broadly enough to cover all paintings, the formula is wide of the mark in other ways. A Constable painting of Marlborough Castle is more like any other picture than it is like the Castle, yet it represents the Castle and not another picture—not even the closest copy. To add the requirement that *B* must not be a picture would be desperate and futile; for a picture may represent another, and indeed each of the once popular paintings of art galleries represents many others.

The plain fact is that a picture, to represent an object,[2] must be a symbol for it, stand for it, refer to it; and that no degree of resemblance is sufficient to establish the requisite relationship of reference. Nor is resemblance *necessary* for reference; almost anything may stand for almost anything else. A picture that represents—like a passage that describes—an object refers to and, more particularly, *denotes*[3] it. Denotation is the core of representation and is independent of resemblance.

If the relation between a picture and what it represents is thus assimilated to the relation between a predicate and what it applies to, we must examine the characteristics of representation as a special kind of denotation. What does pictorial denotation have in common with, and how does it differ from, verbal or diagrammatic denotation? One not implausible answer is that resemblance, while no suffi-

---

[2] I use "object" indifferently for anything a picture represents, whether an apple or a battle. A quirk of language makes a represented object a subject.

[3] Not until the next chapter will denotation be distinguished from other varieties of reference.

cient condition for representation, is just the feature that distinguishes representation from denotation of other kinds. Is it perhaps the case that if *A* denotes *B*, then *A* represents *B* just to the extent that *A* resembles *B*? I think even this watered-down and innocuous-looking version of our initial formula betrays a grave misconception of the nature of representation.

2. Imitation

"To make a faithful picture, come as close as possible to copying the object just as it is." This simple-minded injunction baffles me; for the object before me is a man, a swarm of atoms, a complex of cells, a fiddler, a friend, a fool, and much more. If none of these constitute the object as it is, what else might? If all are ways the object is, then none is *the* way the object is.[4] I cannot copy all these

[4] In "The Way the World Is", *Review of Metaphysics*, vol. 14 (1960), pp. 48–56, I have argued that the world is as many ways as it can be truly described, seen, pictured, etc., and that there is no such thing as *the* way the world is. Ryle takes a somewhat similar position (*Dilemmas* [Cambridge, England, Cambridge University Press, 1954], pp. 75–77) in comparing the relation between a table as a perceived solid object and the table as a swarm of atoms with the relation between a college library according to the catalogue and according to the accountant. Some have proposed that the way the world is could be arrived at by conjoining all the several ways. This overlooks the fact that conjunction itself is peculiar to certain systems; for example, we cannot conjoin a paragraph and a picture. And any attempted combination of all the ways would be itself only one—and a peculiarly indigestible one—of the ways the world is. But what is *the world* that is in so many ways? To speak of ways the world is, or ways of describing or picturing the world, is to speak of world-descriptions or world-pictures, and does not imply there is a unique thing—or indeed

at once; and the more nearly I succeeded, the less would the result be a realistic picture.

What I am to copy then, it seems, is one such aspect, one of the ways the object is or looks. But not, of course, any one of these at random—not, for example, the Duke of Wellington as he looks to a drunk through a raindrop. Rather, we may suppose, the way the object looks to the normal eye, at proper range, from a favorable angle, in good light, without instrumentation, unprejudiced by affections or animosities or interests, and unembellished by thought or interpretation. In short, the object is to be copied as seen under aseptic conditions by the free and innocent eye.

The catch here, as Ernest Gombrich insists, is that there is no innocent eye.[5] The eye comes always ancient to its work, obsessed by its own past and by old and new insinuations of the ear, nose, tongue, fingers, heart, and brain. It functions not as an instrument self-powered and alone, but as a dutiful member of a complex and capricious organism. Not only how but what it sees is regulated by need and prejudice.[6] It selects, rejects, organizes, discriminates, as-

---

anything—that is described or pictured. Of course, none of this implies, either, that nothing is described or pictured. See further section 5 and note 19 below.

[5] In *Art and Illusion* (New York, Pantheon Books, 1960), pp. 297–298 and elsewhere. On the general matter of the relativity of vision, see also such works as R. L. Gregory, *Eye and Brain* (New York, McGraw-Hill Book Co., 1966), and Marshall H. Segall, Donald Campbell, and Melville J. Herskovits, *The Influence of Culture on Visual Perception* (Indianapolis and New York, The Bobbs-Merrill Co., Inc., 1966).

[6] For samples of psychological investigation of this point, see Jerome S. Bruner's "On Perceptual Readiness", *Psychological Review*, vol. 64 (1957), pp. 123–152, and other articles there cited; also William P.

sociates, classifies, analyzes, constructs. It does not so much mirror as take and make; and what it takes and makes it sees not bare, as items without attributes, but as things, as food, as people, as enemies, as stars, as weapons. Nothing is seen nakedly or naked.

The myths of the innocent eye and of the absolute given are unholy accomplices. Both derive from and foster the idea of knowing as a processing of raw material received from the senses, and of this raw material as being discoverable either through purification rites or by methodical disinterpretation. But reception and interpretation are not separable operations; they are thoroughly interdependent. The Kantian dictum echoes here: the innocent eye is blind and the virgin mind empty. Moreover, what has been received and what has been done to it cannot be distinguished within the finished product. Content cannot be extracted by peeling off layers of comment.[7]

All the same, an artist may often do well to strive for innocence of eye. The effort sometimes rescues him from the tired patterns of everyday seeing, and results in fresh insight. The opposite effort, to give fullest rein to a personal reading, can be equally tonic—and for the same rea-

---

Brown, "Conceptions of Perceptual Defense", *British Journal of Psychology Monograph Supplement XXXV* (Cambridge, England, Cambridge University Press, 1961).

[7] On the emptiness of the notion of epistemological primacy and the futility of the search for the absolute given, see my *Structure of Appearance* (2nd edition; Indianapolis and New York, The Bobbs-Merrill Co., Inc., 1966—hereinafter referred to as *SA*), pp. 132–145, and "Sense and Certainty", *Philosophical Review*, vol. 61 (1952), pp. 160–167.

son. But the most neutral eye and the most biased are merely sophisticated in different ways. The most ascetic vision and the most prodigal, like the sober portrait and the vitriolic caricature, differ not in how *much* but only in *how* they interpret.

The copy theory of representation, then, is stopped at the start by inability to specify what is to be copied. Not an object the way it is, nor all the ways it is, nor the way it looks to the mindless eye. Moreover, something is wrong with the very notion of copying any of the ways an object is, any aspect of it. For an aspect is not just the object-from-a-given-distance-and-angle-and-in-a-given-light; it is the object as we look upon or conceive it, a version or construal of the object. In representing an object, we do not copy such a construal or interpretation—we *achieve* it.[8]

In other words, nothing is ever represented either shorn of or in the fullness of its properties. A picture never merely represents *x*, but rather represents *x as* a man or represents *x to be* a mountain, or represents *the fact that x is* a melon. What could be meant by copying a fact would be hard to grasp even if there were any such things as facts; to ask me to copy *x* as a soandso is a little like asking me to sell something as a gift; and to speak of copying something to be a man is sheer nonsense. We shall presently have to look further into all this; but we hardly need

---

[8] And this is no less true when the instrument we use is a camera rather than a pen or brush. The choice and handling of the instrument participate in the construal. A photographer's work, like a painter's, can evince a personal style. Concerning the 'corrections' provided for in some cameras, see section 3 below.

look further to see how little is representation a matter of imitation.

The case for the relativity of vision and of representation has been so conclusively stated elsewhere that I am relieved of the need to argue it at any length here. Gombrich, in particular, has amassed overwhelming evidence to show how the way we see and depict depends upon and varies with experience, practice, interests, and attitudes. But on one matter Gombrich and others sometimes seem to me to take a position at odds with such relativity; and I must therefore discuss briefly the question of the conventionality of perspective.

3. Perspective

An artist may choose his means of rendering motion, intensity of light, quality of atmosphere, vibrancy of color, but if he wants to represent space correctly, he must—almost anyone will tell him—obey the laws of perspective. The adoption of perspective during the Renaissance is widely accepted as a long stride forward in realistic depiction. The laws of perspective are supposed to provide absolute standards of fidelity that override differences in style of seeing and picturing. Gombrich derides "the idea that perspective is merely a convention and does not represent the world as it looks", and he declares "One cannot insist enough that the art of perspective aims at a correct equation: It wants the image to appear like the object and the object like the image." [9] And James J. Gib-

[9] *Art and Illusion*, pp. 254 and 257.

I,3

son writes: ". . . it does not seem reasonable to assert that the use of perspective in paintings is merely a convention, to be used or discarded by the painter as he chooses, . . . When the artist transcribes what he sees upon a two-dimensional surface, he uses perspective geometry, of necessity." [10]

Obviously the laws of the behavior of light are no more conventional than any other scientific laws. Now suppose we have a motionless, monochromatic object, reflecting light of medium intensity only. The argument runs [11]:—A picture drawn in correct perspective will, under specified conditions, deliver to the eye a bundle of light rays matching that delivered by the object itself. This matching is a purely objective matter, measurable by instruments. And such matching constitutes fidelity of representation; for since light rays are all that the eye can receive from either picture or object, identity in pattern of light rays must constitute identity of appearance. Of course, the rays yielded by the picture under the specified conditions match not only those yielded by the object in question from a given distance and angle but also those yielded by

[10] From "Pictures, Perspective, and Perception", *Daedalus* (Winter 1960), p. 227. Gibson does not appear to have explicitly retracted these statements, though his interesting recent book, *The Senses Considered as Perceptual Systems* (Boston, Houghton Mifflin Co., 1966), deals at length with related problems.

[11] Substantially this argument has, of course, been advanced by many other writers. For an interesting discussion see D. Gioseffi, *Perspetiva Artificialis* (Trieste, Universita degli studi di Trieste, Instituto di Storia dell'Arte Antica e Moderna, 1957), and a long review of the same by M. H. Pirenne in *The Art Bulletin*, vol. 41 (1959), pp. 213–217. I am indebted to Professor Meyer Schapiro for this reference.

any of a multitude of other objects from other distances and angles.[12] Identity in pattern of light rays, like resemblance of other kinds, is clearly no sufficient condition for representation. The claim is rather that such identity is a criterion of fidelity, of correct pictorial representation, where denotation is otherwise established.

If at first glance the argument as stated seems simple and persuasive, it becomes less so when we consider the conditions of observation that are prescribed. The picture must be viewed through a peephole, face on, from a certain distance, with one eye closed and the other motionless. The object also must be observed through a peephole, from a given (but not usually the same) angle and distance, and with a single unmoving eye. Otherwise, the light rays will not match.

Under these remarkable conditions, do we not have ultimately faithful representation? Hardly. Under these conditions, what we are looking at tends to disappear rather promptly. Experiment has shown that the eye cannot see normally without moving relative to what it sees [13]; apparently, scanning is necessary for normal vision. The

[12] Cf. Gombrich's discussion of 'gates' in *Art and Illusion*, pp. 250–251.

[13] See L. A. Riggs, F. Ratliff, J. C. Cornsweet, and T. Cornsweet, "The Disappearance of Steadily Fixated Visual Objects", *Journal of the Optical Society of America*, vol. 43 (1953), pp. 495–501. More recently, the drastic and rapid changes in perception that occur during fixation have been investigated in detail by R. M. Pritchard, W. Heron, and D. O. Hebb in "Visual Perception Approached by the Method of Stabilized Images", *Canadian Journal of Psychology*, vol. 14 (1960), pp. 67–77. According to this article, the image tends to regenerate, sometimes transformed into meaningful units not initially present.

fixed eye is almost as blind as the innocent one. What can the matching of light rays delivered under conditions that make normal vision impossible have to do with fidelity of representation? To measure fidelity in terms of rays directed at a closed eye would be no more absurd. But this objection need not be stressed; perhaps enough eye motion could be allowed for scanning but not for seeing around the object.[14] The basic trouble is that the specified conditions of observation are grossly abnormal. What can be the grounds for taking the matching of light rays delivered under such extraordinary conditions as a measure of fidelity? Under no more artificial conditions, such as the interposition of suitably contrived lenses, a picture far out of perspective could also be made to yield the same pattern of light rays as the object. That with clever enough stage-managing we can wring out of a picture drawn in perspective light rays that match those we can wring out of the object represented is an odd and futile argument for the fidelity of perspective.

Furthermore, the conditions of observation in question are in most cases not the same for picture and object. Both are to be viewed through a peephole with one transfixed eye; but the picture is to be viewed face on at a distance of six feet while the cathedral represented has to be looked at from, say, an angle of 45° to its façade and at a distance of two hundred feet. Now not only the light rays received but also the attendant conditions determine what and how

[14] But note that owing to the protuberance of the cornea, the eye when rotated, even with the head fixed, can often see slightly around the sides of an object.

we see; as psychologists are fond of saying, there is more to vision than meets the eye. Just as a red light says "stop" on the highway and "port" at sea, so the same stimulus gives rise to different visual experience under different circumstances. Even where both the light rays and the momentary external conditions are the same, the preceding train of visual experience, together with information gathered from all sources, can make a vast difference in what is seen. If not even the former conditions are the same, duplication of light rays is no more likely to result in identical perception than is duplication of the conditions if the light rays differ.

Pictures are normally viewed framed against a background by a person free to walk about and to move his eyes. To paint a picture that will under these conditions deliver the same light rays as the object, viewed under any conditions, would be pointless even if it were possible. Rather, the artist's task in representing an object before him is to decide what light rays, under gallery conditions, will succeed in rendering what he sees. This is not a matter of copying but of conveying. It is more a matter of 'catching a likeness' than of duplicating—in the sense that a likeness lost in a photograph may be caught in a carica-ture. Translation of a sort, compensating for differences in circumstances, is involved. How this is best carried out depends upon countless and variable factors, not least among them the particular habits of seeing and represent-ing that are ingrained in the viewers. Pictures in perspec-tive, like any others, have to be read; and the ability to read has to be acquired. The eye accustomed solely to Oriental painting does not immediately understand a picture in perspective. Yet with practice one can accommodate smoothly to distorting spectacles or to pictures drawn in warped or even reversed perspective.[15] And even we who are most inured to perspective rendering do not always accept it as faithful representation: the photograph of a man with his feet thrust forward looks distorted, and Pike's Peak dwindles dismally in a snapshot. As the saying goes, there is nothing like a camera to make a molehill out of a mountain.

So far, I have been playing along with the idea that pictorial perspective obeys laws of geometrical optics, and

[15] Adaptation to spectacles of various kinds has been the subject of extensive experimentation. See, for example, J. E. Hochberg, "Effects of Gestalt Revolution: The Cornell Symposium on Perception", *Psychological Review*, vol. 64 (1959), pp. 74–75; J. G. Taylor, *The Behavioral Basis of Perception* (New Haven, Yale University Press, 1962), pp. 166–185; and Irvin Rock, *The Nature of Perceptual Adaptation* (New York, Basic Books, Inc., 1966). Anyone can readily verify for himself how easy it is to learn to read pictures drawn in reversed or otherwise transformed perspective. Reversed perspective often occurs in Oriental, Byzantine, and mediaeval art; sometimes standard and reversed perspective are even used in different parts of one picture—see, for example, Leonid Ouspensky and Vladimir Lossky, *The Meaning of Icons* (Boston, Boston Book and Art Shop, 1952), p. 42 (note 1), p. 200. Concerning the fact that one has to learn to read pictures in standard perspective, Melville J. Herskovits writes in *Man and His Works* (New York, Alfred A. Knopf, 1948), p. 381: "More than one ethnographer has reported the experience of showing a clear photograph of a house, a person, a familiar landscape to people living in a culture innocent of any knowledge of photography, and to have the picture held at all possible angles, or turned over for an inspection of its blank back, as the native tried to interpret this meaningless arrangement of varying shades of grey on a piece of paper. For even the clearest photograph is only an interpretation of what the camera sees."

that a picture drawn according to the standard pictorial rules will, under the very abnormal conditions outlined above, deliver a bundle of light rays matching that delivered by the scene portrayed. Only this assumption gives any plausibility at all to the argument from perspective; but the assumption is plainly false. By the pictorial rules, railroad tracks running outward from the eye are drawn converging, but telephone poles (or the edges of a façade) running upward from the eye are drawn parallel. By the 'laws of geometry' the poles should also be drawn converging. But so drawn, they look as wrong as railroad tracks drawn parallel. Thus we have cameras with tilting backs and elevating lens-boards to 'correct distortion'— that is, to make vertical parallels come out parallel in our photographs; we do not likewise try to make the railroad tracks come out parallel. The rules of pictorial perspective no more follow from the laws of optics than would rules calling for drawing the tracks parallel and the poles converging. In diametric contradiction to what Gibson says, the artist who wants to produce a spatial representation that the present-day Western eye will accept as faithful must defy the 'laws of geometry'.

If all this seems quite evident, and neatly clinched by Klee,[16] there is nevertheless impressive weight of authority on the other side,[17] relying on the argument that

[16] See the frontispiece to this chapter. As Klee remarks, the drawing looks quite normal if taken as representing a floor but awry as representing a façade, even though in the two cases parallels in the object represented recede equally from the eye.

[17] Indeed, this is the orthodox position, taken not only by Pirenne, Gibson, and Gombrich, but by most writers on the subject. Some

PERSPECTIVE

all parallels in the plane of the façade project geometrically as parallels onto the parallel plane of the picture. The source of unending debate over perspective seems to lie in confusion concerning the pertinent conditions of observation. In Figure 1, an observer is on ground level with eye at *a*; at *b,c* is the façade of a tower atop a building; at *d,e* is a picture of the tower façade, drawn in standard perspective and to a scale such that at the indicated distances picture and façade subtend equal angles from *a*. The normal line of vision to the tower is the line *a,f;* looking much higher or lower will leave part of the tower façade out of sight or blurred. Likewise, the normal line of vision to the picture is *a,g*. Now although picture and façade are parallel, the line *a,g* is perpendicular to the picture, so that vertical parallels in the picture will be projected to the eye as parallel, while the line *a,f* is at an angle to the façade so that vertical parallels there will be projected to the eye as converging upward. We might try to make picture and façade deliver matching bundles of light rays to the eye by either (1) moving the picture upward to the position *h,i,* or (2) tilting it to the position *j,k,* or (3) looking at the picture from *a* but at the tower from *m*, some stories up.

exceptions, besides Klee, are Erwin Panofsky, "Die Perspektive als 'Symbolische Form' ", *Vortrage der Bibliothek Warburg* (1924–1925), pp. 258ff; Rudolf Arnheim, *Art and Visual Perception* (Berkeley, University of California Press, 1954), e.g., pp. 92ff, 226ff, and elsewhere; and in an earlier day, one Arthur Parsey, who was taken to task for his heterodox views by Augustus de Morgan in *Budget of Paradoxes* (London, 1872), pp. 176–177. I am indebted to Mr. P. T. Geach for this last reference. Interesting discussions of perspective will be found in *The Birth and Rebirth of Pictorial Space*, by John White (New York, Thomas Yoseloff, 1958), Chapters VIII and XIII.

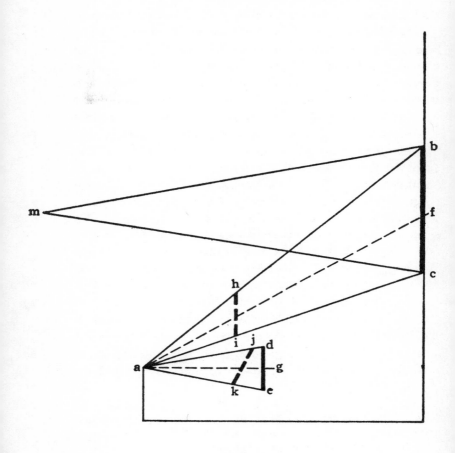

Figure 1

In the first two cases, since the picture must be also nearer the eye to subtend the same angle, the scale will be wrong for lateral (left-right) dimensions. What is more important, none of these three conditions of observation is anywhere near normal. We do not usually hang pictures far above eye level, or tilt them drastically bottom toward us, or elevate ourselves at will to look squarely at towers.[18] With eye and picture in normal position, the bundle of light rays delivered to the eye by the picture drawn in standard perspective is very different from the bundle delivered by the façade.

This argument by itself is conclusive, but my case does not rest upon it. The more fundamental arguments advanced earlier would apply with full force even had the choice of official rules of perspective been less whimsical and called for drawing as convergent all parallels receding in any direction. Briefly, the behavior of light sanctions neither our usual nor any other way of rendering space; and perspective provides no absolute or independent standard of fidelity.

4. Sculpture

The troubles with the copy theory are sometimes attributed solely to the impossibility of depicting reality-in-the-round on a flat surface. But imitation is no better

[18] The optimal way of seeing the tower façade may be by looking straight at it from *m*; but then the optimal way of seeing the railroad tracks would be by looking down on them from directly above the midpoint of their length.

gauge of realism in sculpture than in painting. What is to be portrayed in a bronze bust is a mobile, many-faceted, and fluctuating person, encountered in ever changing light and against miscellaneous backgrounds. Duplicating the form of the head at a given instant is unlikely to yield a notably faithful representation. The very fixation of such a momentary phase embalms the person much as a photograph taken at too short an exposure freezes a fountain or stops a racehorse. To portray faithfully is to convey a person known and distilled from a variety of experiences. This elusive conceit is nothing that one can meaningfully try to duplicate or imitate in a static bronze on a pedestal in a museum. The sculptor undertakes, rather, a subtle and intricate problem of translation.

Even where the object represented is something simpler and more stable than a person, duplication seldom coincides with realistic representation. If in a tympanum over a tall Gothic portal, Eve's apple were the same size as a Winesap, it would not look big enough to tempt Adam. The distant or colossal sculpture has also to be *shaped* very differently from what it depicts in order to be realistic, in order to 'look right'. And the ways of making it 'look right' are not reducible to fixed and universal rules; for how an object looks depends not only upon its orientation, distance, and lighting, but upon all we know of it and upon our training, habits, and concerns.

One need hardly go further to see that the basic case against imitation as a test of realism is conclusive for sculpture as well as for painting.

5. Fictions

So far, I have been considering only the representation of a particular person or group or thing or scene; but a picture, like a predicate, may denote severally the members of a given class. A picture accompanying a definition in a dictionary is often such a representation, not denoting uniquely some one eagle, say, or collectively the class of eagles, but distributively eagles in general.

Other representations have neither unique nor multiple denotation. What, for example, do pictures of Pickwick or of a unicorn represent? They do not represent anything; they are representations with null denotation. Yet how can we say that a picture represents Pickwick, or a unicorn, and also say that it does not represent anything? Since there is no Pickwick and no unicorn, what a picture of Pickwick and a picture of a unicorn represent is the same. Yet surely to be a picture of Pickwick and to be a picture of a unicorn are not at all the same.

The simple fact is that much as most pieces of furniture are readily sorted out as desks, chairs, tables, etc., so most pictures are readily sorted out as pictures of Pickwick, of Pegasus, of a unicorn, etc., without reference to anything represented. What tends to mislead us is that such locutions as "picture of" and "represents" have the appearance of mannerly two-place predicates and can sometimes be so interpreted. But "picture of Pickwick" and "represents a unicorn" are better considered unbreakable one-place predicates, or class-terms, like "desk" and "table". We cannot reach inside any of these and quantify over parts of them. From the fact that P is a picture of or represents a unicorn we cannot infer that there is something that P is a picture of or represents. Furthermore, a picture of Pickwick is a picture of a man, even though there is no man it represents. Saying that a picture represents a soandso is thus highly ambiguous as between saying what the picture denotes and saying what kind of picture it is. Some confusion can be avoided if in the latter case we speak rather of a 'Pickwick-representing-picture' or a 'unicorn-representing-picture' or a 'man-representing-picture' or, for short, of a 'Pickwick-picture' or 'unicorn-picture' or 'man-picture'. Obviously a picture cannot, barring equivocation, both represent Pickwick and represent nothing. But a picture may be of a certain kind—be a Pickwick-picture or a man-picture—without representing anything.[19]

[19] The substance of this and the following two paragraphs is contained in my paper, "On Likeness of Meaning", *Analysis,* vol. 1 (1949), pp. 1–7, and discussed further in the sequel, "On Some Differences about Meaning", *Analysis,* vol. 13 (1953), pp. 90–96. See also the parallel treatment of the problem of statements 'about fictive entities' in "About", *Mind,* vol. 70 (1961), esp. pp. 18–22. In a series of papers from 1939 on (many of them reworked and republished in *From a Logical Point of View* [Cambridge, Mass., Harvard University Press, 1953]), W. V. Quine had sharpened the distinction between syncategorematic and other expressions, and had shown that careful observance of this distinction could dispel many philosophical problems.

I use the device of hyphenation (e.g., in "man-picture") as an aid in technical discourse only, not as a reform of everyday usage, where the context normally prevents confusion and where the impetus to fallacious existential inference is less compulsive, if not less consequential, than in philosophy. In what follows, "man-picture" will always be an abbreviation for the longer and more usual "picture representing a man", taken as an unbreakable one-place predicate that

The difference between a man-picture and a picture of a man has a close parallel in the difference between a man-description (or man-term) and a description of (or term for) a man. "Pickwick", "the Duke of Wellington", "the man who conquered Napoleon", "a man", "a fat man", "the man with three heads", are all man-descriptions, but not all describe a man. Some denote a particular man, some denote each of many men, and some denote nothing.[20] And although "Pickwick" and "the three-headed man" and "Pegasus" all have the same null extension, the second differs from the first in being, for example, a many-headed-man-description, while the last differs from the other two in being a winged-horse-description.

The way pictures and descriptions are thus classified into kinds, like most habitual ways of classifying, is far from sharp or stable, and resists codification. Borderlines shift and blur, new categories are always coming into prominence, and the canons of the classification are less clear than the practice. But this is only to say that we

---

need not apply to all or only to pictures that represent an actual man. The same general principle will govern use of all compounds of the form "——picture". Thus, for example, I shall not use "Churchill-picture" as an abbreviation for "picture painted by Churchill" or for "picture belonging to Churchill". Note, furthermore, that a square-picture is not necessarily a square picture but a square-representing-picture.

[20] Strictly, we should speak here of utterances and inscriptions; for different instances of the same term may differ in denotation. Indeed, classifying replicas together to constitute terms is only one, and a far from simple, way of classifying utterances and inscriptions into kinds. See further *SA*, pp. 359–363, and also Chapter IV below.

may have some trouble in telling whether certain pictures (in common parlance) 'represent a unicorn', or in setting forth rules for deciding in every case whether a picture is a man-picture. Exact and general conditions under which something is a soandso-picture or a soandso-description would indeed be hard to formulate. We can cite examples: Van Gogh's *Postman* is a man-picture; and in English, "a man" is a man-description. And we may note, for instance, that to be a soandso-picture is to be a soandso-picture as a whole, so that a picture containing or contained in a man-picture need not itself be a man-picture. But to attempt much more is to become engulfed in a notorious philosophical morass; and the frustrating, if fascinating, problems involved are no part of our present task. All that directly matters here, I repeat, is that pictures are indeed sorted with varying degrees of ease into man-pictures, unicorn-pictures, Pickwick-pictures, winged-horse-pictures, etc., just as pieces of furniture are sorted into desks, tables, chairs, etc. And this fact is unaffected by the difficulty, in either case, of framing definitions for the several classes or eliciting a general principle of classification.

The possible objection that we must first understand what a man or a unicorn is in order to know how to apply "man-picture" or "unicorn-picture" seems to me quite perverted. We can learn to apply "corncob pipe" or "staghorn" without first understanding, or knowing how to apply, "corn" or "cob" or "corncob" or "pipe" or "stag" or "horn" as separate terms. And we can learn, on the basis of samples, to apply "unicorn-picture" not only without ever having seen any unicorns but without ever having seen or heard the word "unicorn" before. Indeed, largely by learning what are unicorn-pictures and unicorn-descriptions do we come to understand the word "unicorn"; and our ability to recognize a staghorn may help us to recognize a stag when we see one. We may begin to understand a term by learning how to apply either the term itself or some larger term containing it. Acquiring any of these skills may aid in acquiring, but does not imply possessing, any of the others. Understanding a term is not a precondition, and may often be a result, of learning how to apply the term and its compounds.[21]

Earlier I said that denotation is a necessary condition for representation, and then encountered representations without denotation. But the explanation is now clear. A picture must denote a man to represent him, but need not denote anything to be a man-representation. Incidentally, the copy theory of representation takes a further beating here; for where a representation does not represent anything there can be no question of resemblance to what it represents.

Use of such examples as Pickwick-pictures and unicorn-

---

[21] To know how to apply all compounds of a term would entail knowing how to apply at least some compounds of all other terms in the language. We normally say we understand a term when we know reasonably well how to apply it and enough of its more usual compounds. If for a given "——picture" compound we are in doubt about how to apply it in a rather high percentage of cases, this is also true of the correlative "represents as a ——" predicate. Of course, understanding a term is not exclusively a matter of knowing how to apply it and its compounds; such other factors enter as knowing what inferences can be drawn from and to statements containing the term.

pictures may suggest that representations with null denotation are comparatively rare. Quite the contrary; the world of pictures teems with anonymous fictional persons, places, and things. The man in Rembrandt's *Landscape with a Huntsman* is presumably no actual person; he is just the man in Rembrandt's etching. In other words, the etching represents no man but is simply a man-picture, and more particularly a the-man-in-Rembrandt's-*Landscape-with-a-Huntsman*-picture. And even if an actual man be depicted here, his identity matters as little as the artist's blood-type. Furthermore, the information needed to determine what if anything is denoted by a picture is not always accessible. We may, for example, be unable to tell whether a given representation is multiple, like an eagle-picture in the dictionary, or fictive, like a Pickwick-picture. But where we cannot determine whether a picture denotes anything or not, we can only proceed as if it did not—that is, confine ourselves to considering what kind of picture it is. Thus cases of indeterminate denotation are treated in the same way as cases of null denotation.

But not only where the denotation is null or indeterminate does the classification of a picture need to be considered. For the denotation of a picture no more determines its kind than the kind of picture determines the denotation. Not every man-picture represents a man, and conversely not every picture that represents a man is a man-picture. And in the difference between being and not being a man-picture lies the difference, among pictures that denote a man, between those that do and those that do not represent him as a man.

6. Representation-as

The locution "represents . . . as" has two quite different uses. To say that a picture represents the Duke of Wellington as an infant, or as an adult, or as the victor at Waterloo is often merely to say that the picture represents the Duke at a given time or period—that it denotes a certain (long or short, continuous or broken) temporal part or 'time-slice' of him. Here "as . . ." combines with the *noun* "the Duke of Wellington" to form a description of one portion of the whole extended individual.[22] Such a description can always be replaced by another like "the infant Duke of Wellington" or "the Duke of Wellington upon the occasion of his victory at Waterloo". Thus these cases raise no difficulty; all that is being said is that the picture represents the object so described.

The second use is illustrated when we say that a given picture represents Winston Churchill as an infant, where the picture does not represent the infant Churchill but rather represents the adult Churchill as an infant. Here, as well as when we say that other pictures represent the adult Churchill as an adult, the "as . . ." combines with and modifies the *verb*; and we have genuine cases of *representation-as*. Such representation-as wants now to be distinguished from and related to representation.

A picture that represents a man denotes him; a picture

[22] I am indebted to Mr. H. P. Grice and Mr. J. O. Urmson for comments leading to clarification of this point. Sometimes, the portion in question may be marked off along other than temporal lines. On the notion of a temporal part, see *SA*, pp. 127–129.

that represents a fictional man is a man-picture; and a picture that represents a man as a man is a man-picture denoting him. Thus while the first case concerns only what the picture denotes, and the second only what kind of picture it is, the third concerns both the denotation and the classification.

More accurate formulation takes some care. What a picture is said to represent may be denoted by the picture as a whole or by a part of it. Likewise, a picture may be a soandso-picture as a whole or merely through containing a soandso-picture.[23] Consider an ordinary portrait of the Duke and Duchess of Wellington. The picture (as a whole) denotes the couple, and (in part) denotes the Duke. Furthermore, it is (as a whole) a two-person-picture, and (in part) a man-picture. The picture represents the Duke and Duchess as two persons, and represents the Duke as a man. But although it represents the Duke, and is a two-person-picture, it obviously does not represent the Duke as two persons; and although it represents two persons and is a man-picture, it does not represent the two as a man. For the picture neither is nor contains any picture that as a whole both represents the Duke and is a two-man-picture, or that as a whole both represents two persons and is a man-picture.

In general, then, an object k is represented as a soandso by a picture p if and only if p is or contains a picture that

[23] The contained picture may, nevertheless, denote given objects and be a soandso-picture *as a result* of its incorporation in the context of the containing picture, just as "triangle" through occurrence in "triangle and drums" may denote given musical instruments and be a musical-instrument-description.

as a whole both denotes k and is a soandso-picture.[24] Many of the modifiers that have had to be included here may, however, be omitted as understood in what follows; for example, "is or contains a picture that as a whole both denotes Churchill and is an adult-picture" may be shortened to "is an adult-picture denoting Churchill".

Everyday usage is often careless about the distinction between representation and representation-as. Cases have already been cited where in saying that a picture represents a soandso we mean not that it denotes a soandso but that it is a soandso-picture. In other cases, we may mean both. If I tell you I have a picture of a certain black horse, and then I produce a snapshot in which he has come out a light speck in the distance, you can hardly convict me of lying; but you may well feel that I misled you. You understandably took me to mean a picture of the black horse as such; and you therefore expected the picture not only to denote the horse in question but to be a black-horse-picture. Not inconceivably, saying a picture represents the black horse might on other occasions mean that it represents the horse as black (i.e., that it is a black-thing-picture denoting the horse) or that it represents the black thing in question as a horse (i.e., that it is a horse-picture denoting the black thing).

The ambiguities of ordinary use do not end there. To

---

[24] This covers cases where k is represented as a soandso by either a whole picture or part of it. As remarked in the latter part of note 19 above, there are restrictions upon the admissible replacements for "soandso" in this definitional schema; an old or square picture or one belonging to Churchill does not thereby represent him as old or square or self-possessed.

say that the adult Churchill is represented as an infant (or as an adult) is to say that the picture in question is an infant-picture (or an adult-picture). But to say that Pickwick is represented as a clown (or as Don Quixote) cannot mean that the picture is a clown-picture (or Don-Quixote-picture) representing Pickwick; for there is no Pickwick. Rather, what is being said is that the picture belongs to a certain rather narrow class of pictures that may be described as Pickwick-as-clown-pictures (or Pickwick-as-Don-Quixote-pictures).

Distinctions obscured in much informal discourse thus need to be carefully marked for our purposes here. Being a matter of monadic classification, representation-as differs drastically from dyadic denotative representation. If a picture represents *k* as a (or the) soandso, then it denotes *k* and is a soandso-picture. If *k* is identical with *h*, the picture also denotes and represents *h*. And if *k* is a suchandsuch, the picture also represents a (or the) suchandsuch, but not necessarily *as* a (or the) suchandsuch. To represent the first Duke of Wellington is to represent Arthur Wellesley and also to represent a soldier, but not necessarily to represent him *as* a soldier; for some pictures of him are civilian-pictures.

Representations, then, are pictures that function in somewhat the same way as descriptions.[25] Just as objects are classified by means of, or under, various verbal labels,

[25] The reader will already have noticed that "description" in the present text is not confined to what are called definite descriptions in logic but covers all predicates from proper names through purple passages, whether with singular, multiple, or null denotation.

so also are objects classified by or under various pictorial labels. And the labels themselves, verbal or pictorial, are in turn classified under labels, verbal or nonverbal. Objects are classified under "desk", "table", etc., and also under pictures representing them. Descriptions are classified under "desk-description", "centaur-description", "Cicero-name", etc.; and pictures under "desk-picture", "Pickwick-picture", etc. The labeling of labels does not depend upon what they are labels for. Some, like "unicorn", apply to nothing; and as we have noted, not all pictures of soldiers are soldier-pictures. Thus with a picture as with any other label, there are always two questions: what it represents (or describes) and the sort of representation (or description) it is. The first question asks what objects, if any, it applies to as a label; and the second asks about which among certain labels apply to it. In representing, a picture at once picks out a class of objects and belongs to a certain class or classes of pictures.[26]

7. Invention

If representing is a matter of classifying objects rather than of imitating them, of characterizing rather than of copying, it is not a matter of passive reporting. The object does not sit as a docile model with its attributes neatly

[26] The picture does not denote the class picked out, but denotes the no or one or several members of that class. A picture of course belongs to countless classes, but only certain of these (e.g., the class of square-pictures, the class of Churchill-pictures) and not others (e.g., the class of square pictures, the class of pictures belonging to Churchill) have to do with what the picture represents-as.

separated and thrust out for us to admire and portray. It is one of countless objects, and may be grouped with any selection of them; and for every such grouping there is an attribute of the object. To admit all classifications on equal footing amounts to making no classification at all. Classification involves preferment; and application of a label (pictorial, verbal, etc.) as often *effects* as it records a classification. The 'natural' kinds are simply those we are in the habit of picking out for and by labeling. Moreover, the object itself is not ready-made but results from a way of taking the world. The making of a picture commonly participates in making what is to be pictured. The object and its aspects depend upon organization; and labels of all sorts are tools of organization.

Representation and description thus involve and are often involved in organization. A label associates together such objects as it applies to, and is associated with the other labels of a kind or kinds. Less directly, it associates its referents with these other labels and with their referents, and so on. Not all these associations have equal force; their strength varies with their directness, with the specificity of the classifications in question, and with the firmness of foothold these classifications and labelings have secured. But in all these ways a representation or description, by virtue of how it classifies and is classified, may make or mark connections, analyze objects, and organize the world.

Representation or description is apt, effective, illuminating, subtle, intriguing, to the extent that the artist or writer grasps fresh and significant relationships and devises means for making them manifest. Discourse or depiction that marks off familiar units and sorts them into standard sets under well-worn labels may sometimes be serviceable even if humdrum. The marking off of new elements or classes, or of familiar ones by labels of new kinds or by new combinations of old labels, may provide new insight. Gombrich stresses Constable's metaphor: "Painting is a science . . . of which pictures are but the experiments." [27] In representation, the artist must make use of old habits when he wants to elicit novel objects and connections. If his picture is recognized as almost but not quite referring to the commonplace furniture of the everyday world, or if it calls for and yet resists assignment to a usual kind of picture, it may bring out neglected likenesses and differences, force unaccustomed associations, and in some measure remake our world. And if the point of the picture is not only successfully made but is also well-taken, if the realignments it directly and indirectly effects are interesting and important, the picture—like a crucial experiment—makes a genuine contribution to knowledge. To a complaint that his portrait of Gertrude Stein did not look like her, Picasso is said to have answered, "No matter; it will."

In sum, effective representation and description require invention. They are creative. They inform each other; and they form, relate, and distinguish objects. That nature imitates art is too timid a dictum. Nature is a product of art and discourse.

[27] From Constable's fourth lecture at the Royal Institution in 1836; see C. R. Leslie, *Memoirs of the Life of John Constable*, ed. Jonathan Mayne (London, Phaidon Press, 1951), p. 323.

8. Realism

This leaves unanswered the minor question what constitutes realism of representation. Surely not, in view of the
foregoing, any sort of resemblance to reality. Yet we do in
fact compare representations with respect to their realism
or naturalism or fidelity. If resemblance is not the criterion, what is?

One popular answer is that the test of fidelity is deception, that a picture is realistic just to the extent that it is a
successful illusion, leading the viewer to suppose that it is,
or has the characteristics of, what it represents. The proposed measure of realism, in other words, is the probability of confusing the representation with the represented. This is some improvement over the copy theory;
for what counts here is not how closely the picture duplicates an object but how far the picture and object, under
conditions of observation appropriate to each, give rise to
the same responses and expectations. Furthermore, the
theory is not immediately confounded by the fact that
fictive representations differ in degree of realism; for even
though there are no centaurs, a realistic picture might deceive me into taking it for a centaur.

Yet there are difficulties. What deceives depends upon
what is observed, and what is observed varies with interests and habits. If the probability of confusion is 1, we no
longer have representation—we have identity. Moreover,
the probability seldom rises noticeably above zero for even
the most guileful *trompe-l'œil* painting seen under ordinary
gallery conditions. For seeing a picture as a picture pre-

cludes mistaking it for anything else; and the appropriate conditions of observation (e.g., framed, against a uniform background, etc.) are calculated to defeat deception. Deception enlists such mischief as a suggestive setting, or a peephole that occludes frame and background. And deception under such nonstandard conditions is no test of realism; for with enough staging, even the most unrealistic picture can deceive. Deception counts less as a measure of realism than as evidence of magicianship, and is a highly atypical mishap. In looking at the most realistic picture, I seldom suppose that I can literally reach into the distance, slice the tomato, or beat the drum. Rather, I recognize the images as signs for the objects and characteristics represented— signs that work instantly and unequivocally without being confused with what they denote. Of course, sometimes where deception does occur—say by a painted window in a mural—we may indeed call the picture realistic; but such cases provide no basis for the usual ordering of pictures in general as more or less realistic.

Thoughts along these lines have led to the suggestion that the most realistic picture is the one that provides the greatest amount of pertinent information. But this hypothesis can be quickly and completely refuted. Consider a realistic picture, painted in ordinary perspective and normal color, and a second picture just like the first except that the perspective is reversed and each color is replaced by its complementary. The second picture, appropriately interpreted, yields exactly the same information as the first. And any number of other drastic but information-preserving transformations are possible. Obviously, realistic and unrealistic pictures may be equally informative; informational yield is no test of realism.

So far, we have not needed to distinguish between fidelity and realism. The criteria considered earlier have been as unsatisfactory for the one as for the other. But we can no longer equate them. The two pictures just described are equally correct, equally faithful to what they represent, provide the same and hence equally true information; yet they are not equally realistic or literal. For a picture to be faithful is simply for the object represented to have the properties that the picture in effect ascribes to it. But such fidelity or correctness or truth is not a sufficient condition for literalism or realism.

The alert absolutist will argue that for the second picture but not the first we need a key. Rather, the difference is that for the first the key is ready at hand. For proper reading of the second picture, we have to discover rules of interpretation and apply them deliberately. Reading of the first is by virtually automatic habit; practice has rendered the symbols so transparent that we are not aware of any effort, of any alternatives, or of making any interpretation at all.[28] Just here, I think, lies the touchstone of realism: not in quantity of information but in how easily it issues. And this depends upon how stereotyped the mode of representation is, upon how commonplace the labels and their uses have become.

[28] Cf. Descartes, *Meditations on the First Philosophy*, trans. E. S. Haldane and G. R. T. Ross (New York, Dover Publications, Inc., 1955), vol. 1, p. 155; also Berkeley, "Essay Towards a New Theory of Vision", in *Works on Vision*, ed. C. M. Turbayne (New York, The Bobbs-Merrill Co., Inc., 1963), p. 42.

REALISM

Realism is relative, determined by the system of representation standard for a given culture or person at a given time. Newer or older or alien systems are accounted artificial or unskilled. For a Fifth-Dynasty Egyptian the straightforward way of representing something is not the same as for an eighteenth-century Japanese; and neither way is the same as for an early twentieth-century Englishman. Each would to some extent have to learn how to read a picture in either of the other styles. This relativity is obscured by our tendency to omit specifying a frame of reference when it is our own. "Realism" thus often comes to be used as the name for a particular style or system of representation. Just as on this planet we usually think of objects as fixed if they are at a constant position in relation to the earth, so in this period and place we usually think of paintings as literal or realistic if they are in a traditional [29] European style of representation. But such egocentric ellipsis must not tempt us to infer that these objects (or any others) are absolutely fixed, or that such pictures (or any others) are absolutely realistic.

Shifts in standard can occur rather rapidly. The very effectiveness that may attend judicious departure from a traditional system of representation sometimes inclines us at least temporarily to install the newer mode as standard. We then speak of an artist's having achieved a new degree of realism, or having found new means for the realistic rendering of (say) light or motion. What happens here is

[29] Or conventional; but "conventional" is a dangerously ambiguous term: witness the contrast between "very conventional" (as "very ordinary") and "highly conventional" or "highly conventionalized" (as "very artificial").

something like the 'discovery' that not the earth but the sun is 'really fixed'. Advantages of a new frame of reference, partly because of their novelty, encourage its enthronement on some occasions in place of the customary frame. Nevertheless, whether an object is 'really fixed' or a picture is realistic depends at any time entirely upon what frame or mode is then standard. Realism is a matter not of any constant or absolute relationship between a picture and its object but of a relationship between the system of representation employed in the picture and the standard system. Most of the time, of course, the traditional system is taken as standard; and the literal or realistic or naturalistic system of representation is simply the customary one.

Realistic representation, in brief, depends not upon imitation or illusion or information but upon inculcation. Almost any picture may represent almost anything; that is, given picture and object there is usually a system of representation, a plan of correlation, under which the picture represents the object.[30] How correct the picture is under that system depends upon how accurate is the information about the object that is obtained by reading the picture according to that system. But how literal or realistic the picture is depends upon how standard the system is. If representation is a matter of choice and correctness a matter of information, realism is a matter of habit.

---

[30] Indeed, there are usually many such systems. A picture that under one (unfamiliar) system is a correct but highly unrealistic representation of an object may under another (the standard) system be a realistic but very incorrect representation of the same object. Only if accurate information is yielded under the standard system will the picture represent the object both correctly and literally.

Our addiction, in the face of overwhelming counter-evidence, to thinking of resemblance as the measure of realism is easily understood in these terms. Representational customs, which govern realism, also tend to generate resemblance. That a picture looks like nature often means only that it looks the way nature is usually painted. Again, what will deceive me into supposing that an object of a given kind is before me depends upon what I have noticed about such objects, and this in turn is affected by the way I am used to seeing them depicted. Resemblance and deceptiveness, far from being constant and independent sources and criteria of representational practice are in some degree products of it.[31]

---

[31] Neither here nor elsewhere have I argued that there is no constant relation of resemblance; judgments of similarity in selected and familiar respects are, even though rough and fallible, as objective and categorical as any that are made in describing the world. But judgments of complex overall resemblance are another matter. In the first place, they depend upon the aspects or factors in terms of which the objects in question are compared; and this depends heavily on conceptual and perceptual habit. In the second place, even with these factors determined, similarities along the several axes are not immediately commensurate, and the degree of total resemblance will depend upon how the several factors are weighted. Normally, for example, nearness in geographical location has little to do with our judgment of resemblance among buildings but much to do with our judgment of resemblance among building lots. The assessment of total resemblance is subject to influences galore, and our representational customs are not least among these. In sum, I have sought to show that insofar as resemblance is a constant and objective relation, resemblance between a picture and what it represents does not coincide with realism; and that insofar as resemblance does coincide with realism, the criteria of resemblance vary with changes in representational practice.

9. Depiction and Description

Throughout, I have stressed the analogy between pictorial representation and verbal description because it seems to me both corrective and suggestive. Reference to an object is a necessary condition for depiction or description of it, but no degree of resemblance is a necessary or sufficient condition for either. Both depiction and description participate in the formation and characterization of the world; and they interact with each other and with perception and knowledge. They are ways of classifying by means of labels having singular or multiple or null reference. The labels, pictorial or verbal, are themselves classified into kinds; and the interpretation of fictive labels, and of depiction-*as* and description-*as*, is in terms of such kinds. Application and classification of a label are relative to a system [32]; and there are countless alternative systems of representation and description. Such systems are the products of stipulation and habituation in varying proportions. The choice among systems is free; but given a system, the question whether a newly encountered object is a desk or a unicorn-picture or is represented by a certain painting is a question of the propriety, under that system, of projecting the predicate "desk" or the predicate "unicorn-picture" or the painting over the thing in question,

---

[32] To anticipate fuller explanation in Chapter V, a symbol system (not necessarily formal) embraces both the symbols and their interpretation, and a language is a symbol system of a particular kind. A formal system is couched in a language and has stated primitives and routes of derivation.

and the decision both is guided by and guides usage for that system.[33]

The temptation is to call a system of depiction a language; but here I stop short. The question what distinguishes representational from linguistic systems needs close examination. One might suppose that the criterion of realism can be made to serve here, too; that symbols grade from the most realistic depictions through less and less realistic ones to descriptions. This is surely not the case; the measure of realism is habituation, but descriptions do not become depictions by habituation. The most commonplace nouns of English have not become pictures.

To say that depiction is by pictures while description is by passages is not only to beg a good part of the question but also to overlook the fact that denotation by a picture does not always constitute depiction; for example, if pictures in a commandeered museum are used by a briefing officer to stand for enemy emplacements, the pictures do not thereby represent these emplacements. To represent, a picture must function as a pictorial symbol; that is, func-

---

[33] On the interaction between specific judgment and general policy, see my *Fact, Fiction, and Forecast* (2nd edition; Indianapolis and New York, The Bobbs-Merrill Co., Inc., 1965—hereinafter referred to as *FFF*), pp. 63–64. The propriety of projecting a predicate might be said to depend upon what similarities there are among the objects in question; but with equal truth, similarities among the objects might be said to depend upon what predicates are projected (cf. note 31 above, and *FFF*, pp. 82, 96–99, 119–120). Concerning the relationship between the 'language theory' of pictures outlined above and the much discussed 'picture theory' of language, see "The Way the World Is" (cited in note 4 above), pp. 55–56.

tion in a system such that what is denoted depends solely upon the pictorial properties of the symbol. The pictorial properties might be roughly delimited by a loose recursive specification.[34] An elementary pictorial characterization states what color a picture has at a given place on its face. Other pictorial characterizations in effect combine many such elementary ones by conjunction, alternation, quantification, etc. Thus a pictorial characterization may name the colors at several places, or state that the color at one place lies within a certain range, or state that the colors at two places are complementary, and so on. Briefly, a pictorial characterization says more or less completely and more or less specifically what colors the picture has at what places. And the properties correctly ascribed to a picture by pictorial characterization are its pictorial properties.

All this, though, is much too special. The formula can easily be broadened a little but resists generalization. Sculptures with denotation dependent upon such sculptural properties as shape do represent, but words with denotation dependent upon such verbal properties as spelling do not. We have not yet captured the crucial difference between pictorial and verbal properties, between nonlinguistic and linguistic symbols or systems, that makes the difference between representation in general and description.

What we have done so far is to subsume representation

---

[34] The specification that follows has many shortcomings, among them the absence of provision for the often three-dimensional nature of picture surfaces. But while a rough distinction between pictorial and other properties is useful here and in some later contexts, nothing very vital rests on its precise formulation.

with description under denotation. Representation is thus disengaged from perverted ideas of it as an idiosyncratic physical process like mirroring, and is recognized as a symbolic relationship that is relative and variable. Furthermore, representation is thus contrasted with non-denotative modes of reference. Some of these will be considered in the following chapter. Only much later shall I come back to the troublesome question of distinguishing representational systems from languages.

red green blue green red yellow blue

yellow red blue yellow green red blue

blue yellow yellow blue red blue yellow

red green green red green green green

green blue blue yellow yellow yellow

yellow red green yellow blue green red

blue green red red green red green blue

red yellow yellow red blue yellow blue

yellow blue red blue green green yellow

green red yellow blue yellow blue red

blue red blue green red yellow blue

green green red yellow blue yellow blue

Reverse

Test Sheet. Adapted from J. R. Stroop (see note 10 below).

II

THE SOUND OF PICTURES

Double sound—cold tension of the straight lines, warm tension of the curved lines, the rigid to the loose, the yielding to the compact.

Wassily Kandinsky*

1. A Difference in Domain

In everyday talk we play at least as fast and loose with the word "express" as with the word "represent". We may say that a statement expresses what it asserts or describes or suggests; that a picture expresses a feeling, a fact, an idea, or a personality. Perhaps the beginning of some order can be imposed on this chaos if a characteristic and peculiar relation of expression, as distinguished from representation and from reference of other kinds in the arts, can be isolated. A first step is to resolve one prevalent ambiguity. That a person expresses sadness may mean that he expresses the feeling of sadness or that he expresses his having of that feeling. This muddles matters, since obviously a person may express sadness he neither has nor claims to have, or may have or claim to have a feeling he does not express. I think we shall do best at the start to

* Caption for a drawing in *Point and Line to Plane*, translated by H. Dearstyne and H. Rebay (New York, Solomon R. Guggenheim Foundation, 1947), pp. 188–189.

45

confine "express" to cases where reference is to a feeling or other property [1] rather than to an occurrence of it. What is involved in showing or affirming that a property is present on a given occasion can be otherwise interpreted. One tentative characteristic difference, then, between representation and expression is that representation is of objects or events, while expression is of feelings or other properties.

Are the two relations distinguished, though, only by what they relate? Brothers and sisters are alike siblings and the difference between being a brother and being a sister depends solely upon whether the sibling is male or female. Is it similarly the case that what is represented and what is expressed are alike denoted, and that the difference depends solely upon whether what is denoted is a particular or a property? Or is there some more radical difference between the two relations?

Offhand, expression may appear to be less literal than representation. Most often the feeling or emotion or property expressed is remote from the medium of expression: a painting may express heat, a musical composition may express color or fragility. Surely any sort of copying is out of the question here. Expression is by intimation rather than by imitation. But we have seen that representation is not imitation either, that no degree of similarity is required between even the most literal picture and what it represents.

---

[1] The seemingly shameless platonism exhibited here will be corrected shortly (section 3 below).

A DIFFERENCE IN DOMAIN

Perhaps, then, a difference is to be sought in the opposite direction: perhaps expression is more direct and immediate than representation. Consonant with this is the
idea that an expression is causally linked with what is expressed. The expression on a face, for example, may be the
effect of the fear or anger or sorrow a person feels, the
facial configurations at once arising from and showing
forth that emotion; or James-Lange-like, the emotion may
arise from perception of the bodily expression. In neither
version will this stand up very long. A pleased expression
may be due to politeness and endured with discomfort;
and fear may give rise to an expression of abject approval
that drains rather than bolsters confidence. An actor's
facial expression need neither result from nor result in his
feeling the corresponding emotions. A painter or composer does not have to have the emotions he expresses in
his work. And obviously works of art themselves do not
feel what they express, even when what they express is a
feeling.

Some of these cases suggest that what is expressed is,
rather, the feeling or emotion excited in the viewer: that a
picture expresses sadness by making the gallery-goer a bit
sad, and a tragedy expresses grief by reducing the spectator to virtual or actual tears. The actor need not feel sad,
but succeeds in expressing sadness just to the extent that he
makes me feel sad. If this view is any more plausible than
the first one considered, it is hardly more defensible. For
one thing, whatever emotion may be excited is seldom the
one expressed. A face expressing agony inspires pity rather
than pain; a body expressing hatred and anger tends to

arouse aversion or fear. Again, what is expressed may be something other than a feeling or emotion. A black and white picture expressing color does not make me feel colorful; and a portrait expressing courage and cleverness hardly produce⌐ ther quality in the viewer.

These confuseu notions of expression are entangled with the popular conviction that excitation of the emotions is a primary function of art. Let me enter here a parenthetical protest against this idea, and against aesthetic theories—such as that of emotional catharsis—dependent upon it. But I shall come back to this later (VI,3–4).

If expression does not differ from representation in being less a matter of imitation or in being more a matter of causation, is expression nevertheless a more nearly absolute and invariable relation? We saw that representation is relative—that any picture may represent any object. In contrast, it seems that a smiling face can hardly express grief, a drooping figure elation, a slate-blue picture express heat, or a staccato and presto passage calm. If the connection is not causal, at least it seems constant. But this distinction evaporates too. When the first fine Japanese films reached us, Western audiences had some difficulty in determining what emotions the actors were expressing. Whether a face was expressing agony or hatred or anxiety or determination or despair or desire was not always instantly evident; for even facial expressions are to some extent molded by custom and culture. What the insular and amateur spectator may take to be instinctive and invariable, the professional actor or director knows to be acquired and variable. If we prejudicially regard the gestures of a foreign dance as highly artificial, and those of our native dances as more innate, the perceptive performer or teacher harbors no such delusions; an eminent choreographer and director writes:

Along the way I have often been obliged to teach young men how to make love, and young girls how to be predatory or flirtatious or seductive, and I've had to advise everybody how to express anxiety, alarm and endless other emotional states. They may have felt these things, but the movements for them are complete strangers.

. . . gestures are patterns of movement established by long usage among men. . . . There are many feelings which can be expressed in so many ways that there is really no one pattern for them. For example, hope has no shape, nor do inspiration, fear, or love.[2]

And the anthropologist concurs:

Insofar as I have been able to determine, just as there are no universal words, sound complexes, which carry the same meaning the world over, there are no body motions, facial expressions or gestures which provoke identical responses the world over. A body can be bowed in grief, in humility, in laughter, or in readiness for aggression. A "smile" in one society portrays friendliness, in another embarrassment and, in still another, may contain a warning that, unless tension is reduced, hostility and attack will follow.[3]

[2] Doris Humphrey, *The Art of Making Dances* (New York, Rinehart & Co., Inc., 1959), pp. 114, 118.

[3] From a talk by Ray L. Birdwhistell, "The Artist, the Scientist and a Smile", given at the Maryland Institute of Art, December 4, 1964.

With representation and expression alike, certain relationships become firmly fixed for certain people by habit; but in neither case are these relationships absolute, universal, or immutable.

So far, then, we have found nothing incompatible with the conclusion that representation and expression are both species of denotation, distinguished only by whether that which is denoted is concrete or abstract. But we must look further.

2. A Difference in Direction

Before me is a picture of trees and cliffs by the sea, painted in dull grays, and expressing great sadness. This description gives information of three kinds, saying something about (1) what things the picture represents, (2) what properties it possesses, and (3) what feelings it expresses. The logical nature of the underlying relationships in the first two cases is plain: the picture denotes a certain scene and is a concrete instance of certain shades of gray. But what is the logical character of the relationship the picture bears to what it is said to express?

A second look at the description may raise some question about the line between possession and expression of a property. For instead of saying the picture expresses sadness I might have said that it is a sad picture. Is it sad, then, in the same way that it is gray? A notable difference is that since, strictly speaking, only sentient beings or events can be sad, a picture is only figuratively sad. A picture literally possesses a gray color, really belongs to the class of gray things; but only metaphorically does it possess sadness or belong to the class of things that feel sad.

Expression, then, can be tentatively and partially characterized as involving figurative possession. This may explain our feeling that expression is somehow both more direct and less literal than representation. For possession seems more intimate than denotation, while the figurative is surely less literal than the literal. Yet to say that expression involves figurative possession seems at once to assimilate it to possession and to contrast it with possession. "Figurative" seems to imply "not actual". In what sense can expression involve possession but not actual possession? Some analysis of the nature of the figurative, or at least of the metaphorical, will have to be undertaken presently; for although what is metaphorically true is not literally true, neither is it merely false. Yet what distinguishes metaphorical truth from literal truth on the one hand and from falsity on the other?

Before going into that question, we had better examine actual possession more closely. An object is gray, or is an instance of or possesses grayness, if and only if "gray" applies to the object.[4] Thus while a picture denotes what it represents, and a predicate denotes what it describes, what properties the picture or the predicate possesses depends rather upon what predicates denote it. A picture cannot be said to denote those properties or predicates except in the upside-down way that a local newspaper was

---

[4] Extensionality is preserved in this formula; truth-value is unaffected when "gray" is replaced by any coextensive predicate.

said to have 'acquired new owners'. The picture *does not denote* the color gray *but is denoted by* the predicate "gray".

Thus if representation is a matter of denotation while expression is somehow a matter of possession, the two differ in direction as well as (or perhaps rather than) in domain. Whether or not what is represented is concrete while what is expressed is abstract, what is expressed subsumes the picture as an instance much as the picture subsumes what it represents.

Expression is not, of course, mere possession. Apart from the fact that the possession involved in expression is metaphorical, neither literal nor metaphorical possession constitutes symbolization at all. To denote is to refer, but to be denoted is not necessarily to refer to anything. Yet expression, like representation, is a mode of symbolization; and a picture must stand for, symbolize, refer to, what it expresses. The symbolization or reference here runs, as we have seen, in the opposite direction from denotation—runs up from rather than down to what is denoted. An object that is literally or metaphorically denoted by a predicate, and refers to that predicate or the corresponding property, may be said to exemplify that predicate or property. Not all exemplification is expression, but all expression is exemplification.

3. Exemplification

Although encountered here rather incidentally in the course of our inquiry into expression, and seldom given much attention, exemplification is an important and widely used mode of symbolization in and out of the arts.

EXEMPLIFICATION

Consider a tailor's booklet of small swatches of cloth. These function as samples, as symbols exemplifying certain properties. But a swatch does not exemplify all its properties; it is a sample of color, weave, texture, and pattern, but not of size, shape, or absolute weight or value. Nor does it even exemplify all the properties—such as having been finished on a Tuesday—that it shares with the given bolt or run of material. Exemplification is possession plus reference.[5] To have without symbolizing is merely to possess, while to symbolize without having is to refer in some other way than by exemplifying. The swatch exemplifies only those properties that it both has and refers to. We may speak of it as exemplifying the bolt or the run in the elliptical sense of exemplifying the property of being from the bolt.[6] But not every piece of the material functions as a sample; and something else such as a painted chip of wood may have, and be used to exemplify, the color or other properties of the material.

If possession is intrinsic, reference is not; and just which properties of a symbol are exemplified depends upon what particular system of symbolization is in effect. The tailor's sample does not normally function as a sample of a tailor's sample; it normally exemplifies certain properties of a ma-

[5] Ostension, like exemplification, has to do with samples; but whereas ostension is the act of pointing to a sample, exemplification is the relation between a sample and what it refers to.

[6] Likewise, to say that a car on the showroom floor exemplifies a Rolls-Royce is to say elliptically that the car exemplifies the property of being a Rolls-Royce. But such ellipsis can be dangerous in technical discourse where to say that x exemplifies a B means that x refers to and is denoted by a B. See further below.

terial, but not the property of exemplifying such properties. Yet if offered in response to a question about what a tailor's sample is, the swatch may indeed exemplify the property of being a tailor's sample. What startles and amuses us in Ring Lardner's remark that one of his stories "is an example of what can be done with a stub pen"[7] is that the story, although it may have the property that its manuscript was written with a stub pen, does not in the context, or in any usual context, exemplify that property.

So far I have spoken indifferently of properties or predicates as being exemplified. This equivocation must now be resolved. Although we usually speak of what is exemplified as redness, or the property of being red, rather than as the predicate "(is) red", this leads to familiar troubles attendant upon any talk of properties. Socrates discussing philosophy in Athens is a rational animal, a featherless biped, and a laughing mammal; but his exemplifying the first property does not imply his exemplifying the other two. Perhaps that is because the three properties, while coextensive, are not identical. But a figure that exemplifies triangularity, though always trilateral, does not always exemplify trilaterality. If trilaterality is not identical with triangularity, what is? And if the two properties are identical, then identical properties may differ in what exemplifies them. We seem to need a different property for every predicate.

Let us, then, take exemplification of *predicates* and

---

[7] In *How to Write Short Stories (with Samples)*, (New York, Charles Scribner's Sons, 1924), p. 247.

other labels as elementary. In so speaking, say of a chip as a
sample of "red" rather than of redness, we must remember
that what exemplifies here is something denoted by, rather
than an inscription of, the predicate. What a symbol exemplifies must apply to it. A man, but not an inscription,
may exemplify (every inscription of) "man"; an inscription, but not a man, may exemplify (every inscription of)
" 'man' ".

Yet to insist that "exemplifies redness" must always be
regarded as a sloppy equivalent of "exemplifies 'red'" is
too strict. To Plato, Socrates hardly exemplified "rational"
but rather the corresponding Greek predicate; and a paint
chip exemplifies "rouge", not "red", to a Frenchman. Even
within English, we may hesitate to say that a sample refers
to one rather than another among alternative predicates.
What we need is an interpretation of "exemplifies redness", in terms of exemplification of predicates, that gives
more latitude.

Suppose we construe "exemplifies redness" as elliptical
for "exemplifies some label coextensive with 'red'". To
say that Socrates exemplifies rationality is, then, to say
only that Socrates exemplifies some label coextensive with
"rational". This provides enough latitude, but seems to
provide too much. For if Socrates exemplifies rationality,
and "rational" is coextensive with "risible", then Socrates
will also exemplify risibility. He *does not*, indeed, therefore
exemplify "risible". But must we choose between an interpretation so wide as to let in risibility and one so narrow
as to shut out the Greek equivalent of "rational"?

The answer is that the lines may be drawn with any

degree of looseness or tightness. While "exemplifies rationality", taken by itself, says only "exemplifies *some* label coextensive with 'rational'", the context usually tells us a good deal more about what label is in question. When a paint chip exemplifies redness to a Frenchman, or Socrates exemplifies rationality to Plato, the predicates are pretty clearly not English ones. In talk among English-speaking people about painting a house, a sample of redness exemplifies "red" or perhaps some or all of a few predicates used interchangeably with "red" in such discussions. In saying that Socrates exemplifies rationality to me, I am surely not saying that he exemplifies a Greek word I do not know. But am I saying he exemplifies "risible"? I may comply with such a request to be more specific about the label or labels exemplified, or I may rest with what amounts to the indefinite statement that Socrates exemplifies some label coextensive with "rational". If I choose the latter course, I am not entitled to complain about the indefiniteness of my answer. In short, we can be as specific or as general as we like about what is exemplified, but we cannot achieve maximum specificity and maximum generality at the same time.

Earlier I said that what is exemplified is abstract. Now I have interpreted exemplification as obtaining between the sample and a label—for instance, between the sample and each concrete inscription of a predicate. Such a label (i.e., its inscriptions) may indeed be 'abstract' in having multiple denotation; but a singular label may equally well be exemplified by what it denotes. And a label, whether with plural or singular or null denotation, may of course be itself denoted. The 'difference in domain' discussed earlier thus reduces to this: while anything may be denoted, only labels may be exemplified.[8]

4. Samples and Labels

Treating all exemplification as fundamentally of labels raises, however, the question whether exemplification is indeed entirely dependent upon language. Does exemplification emerge only as language develops? Are only words exemplified? Are there no samples of anything unnamed? The general answer is that not all labels are predicates; predicates are labels from linguistic systems. Symbols from other systems—gestural, pictorial, diagrammatic, etc. —may be exemplified and otherwise function much as predicates of a language. Such nonlinguistic systems, some of them developed before the advent or acquisition of language, are in constant use. Exemplification of an unnamed property usually amounts to exemplification of a nonverbal symbol for which we have no corresponding word or description.

Yet the orientation that distinguishes exemplification from denotation does seem to derive from the organization of language even where nonverbal symbols are involved. In ordinary language, the reference of "man" to Churchill, and of "word" to "man", is unequivocally denotation; while if

---

[8] If (as in *SA*, Part III) such abstract entities as qualia are recognized, these—although not labels—may indeed be exemplified by their instances, which are concrete wholes containing these qualia. But exemplification of other properties would still have to be explained as above in terms of exemplification of predicates; and simplicity of exposition for our present purposes seems best served by treating all exemplification in this one way.

Churchill symbolizes "man", and "man" symbolizes "word", the reference is unequivocally exemplification. With pictures, although they are nonverbal, orientation of referential relationships is provided by established correlations with language. A picture that represents Churchill, like a predicate that applies to him, denotes him. And reference by a picture to one of its colors often amounts to exemplification of a predicate of ordinary language. Such parallels and points of contact with language are enough to set the direction.

Where there are no such ties to language, and symbols and referents are nonverbal, the distinction in direction between denotation and exemplification is sometimes determinable from formal features. If a diagram of reference is such that all its arrows are single-headed, exemplification is absent; for we know that exemplification implies the converse of denotation. Where double-headed arrows occur, we may be able to tell in which direction denotation runs. For example, if the elements (nodes of the diagram) are antecedently distinguished into two categories, *A* and *B*, and every single-headed arrow runs from an *A* to a *B*, then reference from an *A* to a *B* here is always denotation, reference from a *B* to an *A* exemplification. This general idea can be refined and elaborated to operate in some more complicated cases; but in others the distinction between denotation and exemplification may lose significance. It is pertinent only where there are two dominant opposing directions.

Labeling seems to be free in a way that sampling is not. I can let anything denote red things, but I cannot let anything that is not red be a sample of redness. Is exemplification, then, more intrinsic, less arbitrary, than denotation? The difference amounts to this: for a word, say, to denote red things requires nothing more than letting it refer to them; but for my green sweater to exemplify a predicate, letting the sweater refer to that predicate is not enough. The sweater must also be denoted by that predicate; that is, I must also let the predicate refer to the sweater. The constraint upon exemplification as compared with denotation derives from the status of exemplification as a subrelation of the converse of denotation, from the fact that denotation implies reference between two elements in one direction while exemplification implies reference between the two in both directions. Exemplification is restricted only insofar as the denotation of the label in question is regarded as having been antecedently fixed.

Matters are further complicated by symbols that refer to themselves. A symbol that denotes itself also exemplifies itself, is both denoted and exemplified by itself. "Word" is thus related to itself, and so are "short" and "polysyllabic", but not "long" or "monosyllabic". "Long" is a sample of "short", "monosyllabic" denotes short words, and "short" both exemplifies and denotes short words.[9]

---

[9] Self-reference is a rather mind-twisting matter. The following theorems are noted here for guidance:
(a) If x exemplifies y, then y denotes x.
(b) x and y denote each other if and only if they exemplify each other.
(c) x exemplifies x if and only if x denotes x.
(d) If x exemplifies and is coextensive with y, then x denotes and exemplifies x.

If I ask the color of your house, you may say "red", or you may show me a red paint-chip, or you may write "red" in red ink. You may, that is, respond with a predicate, with a sample, or with a combined predicate and sample. In this last case what you write, taken as a predicate, is interchangeable with any inscription spelled the same way, but taken as a color-sample is interchangeable rather with anything of the same color. The distinction illustrated here becomes important in the translation of poetry or other literature. Original and translation will of course differ in some properties; but so do any two inscriptions of the same word, or even any two red inscriptions of "red". The goal is maximal preservation of what the original *exemplifies* as well as of what it says. Translation of a staccato by a legato text may do greater violence than some discrepancies in denotation. (See section 9 below.)

We are accustomed to taking inscriptions as labels rather than as color-samples, paint-chips as color-samples rather than as labels. But inscriptions may function also as color-samples, as we have just seen and as they do in a disconcerting way when we have to cope, in the frontispiece to this chapter, with several intermixed and differently colored occurrences of "red", "yellow", "blue", and "green".[10] And color-chips may also be used as labels.

---

[10] The interference resulting from the double functioning of such symbols has been investigated experimentally by several psychologists. See J. R. Stroop, "Studies of Interference in Serial Verbal Reactions", *Journal of Experimental Psychology*, vol. 18 (1935), pp. 643–661, and A. R. Jensen and W. D. Rohwer, Jr., "The Stroop Color-Word Test: A Review", *Acta Psychologica*, vol. 25 (1966), pp. 36–93. I am indebted to Paul Kolers for calling my attention to this material.

Each may denote everything of its own color, and will then both exemplify and be the label exemplified[11]; or each may denote only but not all things of its own color, say the buttons in a box; or each may denote things, such as nails of a certain size, regardless of their color.[12]

A gesture, too, may denote or exemplify or both. Nods of agreement or dissent, salutes, bows, pointings, serve as labels. A negative nod, for instance, applies to without normally being among things disapproved. An orchestra conductor's gestures denote sounds to be produced but are not themselves sounds. They may indeed have and even exemplify some properties—say of speed or cadence—of the music, but the gestures are not among their own denotata. The same is true of such activities in response to music as foot- and finger-tappings, head-bobbings, and various other minor motions. That these are called forth by the music, while the conductor's gestures call it forth,

[11] Likewise a sound, in onomatopoeia, may be used to denote sounds having properties it exemplifies. The variability of exemplification is amusingly attested here by some linguistic curiosities: it seems that French dogs bark "gnaf-gnaf" rather than "bow-wow"; that German cats purr "schnurr-schnurr", French cats "ron-ron"; that in Germany a bell goes "bim-bam" rather than "ding-dong", and in France a drip-drip is a plouf-plouf.

[12] That a label is self-exemplifying implies no resemblance to other denotata beyond sharing that predicate. "Material object" denotes itself but is very unlike Windsor Castle. Nor does likeness of a predicate to its denotata imply self-exemplification; for obviously we may use an element to denote those other than itself that resemble it to any degree. Incidentally, though, in judging the similarity of two things we tend to weigh a predicate they exemplify more heavily than one that merely denotes them; for an exemplified predicate is referred to, and thus gains prominence.

does not affect their status as labels; for labels may be used to record or to prescribe—"strawberry", "raspberry", "lemon", and "lime" may tell us what *is* in or what *to put* in the several containers.

Why, though, do these negligible activities become so significant when related to music? Their significance is simply that of labels applied in analyzing, organizing, and registering what we hear. *Contra* theories of empathy,[13] these labels need not themselves have any particular properties in common with the music. Psychologists and linguists have stressed the ubiquitous participation of action in perception in general, the early and extensive use of gestural, sensorimotor, or enactive symbols, and the role of such symbols in cognitive development.[14] For Jaques-

[13] See, for example, Theodor Lipps, *Raumaesthetik und Geometrisch-Optische Täuschungen* (Leipzig, J. A. Barth, 1897), translated by H. S. Langfeld in *The Aesthetic Attitude* (New York, Harcourt, Brace & Co., Inc., 1920), pp. 6–7: "The column seems to brace itself and raise itself, that is to say, to proceed in the way in which I do when I pull myself together and raise myself, or remain thus tense and erect, in opposition to the natural inertness of my body. It is impossible for me to be aware of the column without this activity seeming to exist directly in the column of which I am aware."

[14] See, for example, Burton L. White and Richard Held, "Plasticity of Sensorimotor Development in the Human Infant", in *The Causes of Behavior*, ed. J. F. Rosenblith and W. Allinsmith (2nd ed., Boston, Allyn and Bacon, Inc., 1966), pp. 60–70, and the earlier articles there cited; Ray L. Birdwhistell, "Communication without Words", prepared in 1964 for publication in "L'Aventure Humaine", and the articles there cited; Jean Piaget, *The Origins of Intelligence in Children* (New York, International University Press, Inc., 1952), e.g., pp. 185ff, 385; and Jerome S. Bruner, *Studies in Cognitive Growth* (New York, John Wiley & Sons, Inc., 1966), pp. 12–21. I cannot accept

Dalcroze, the use of these activities for grasping music is a fundamental factor in musical education.[15]

The gymnastics instructor, unlike the orchestra conductor, gives samples. His demonstrations exemplify the requisite properties of the actions to be performed by his class, whereas his oral instructions prescribe rather than show what is to be done. The proper response to his knee-bend is a knee-bend; the proper response to his shout "lower" (even if in a high voice) is not to shout "lower" but to bend deeper. Nevertheless, since the demonstrations are part of the instruction, are accompanied by and may be replaced by verbal directions, and have no already established denotation, they may—like any sample not otherwise committed as to denotation—also be taken as denoting what the predicates they exemplify denote, and are then labels exemplifying themselves.

The action of a mime, on the other hand, is not usually among the actions it denotes. He does not climb ladders or wash windows but rather portrays, represents, denotes,

---

Bruner's trichotomy of symbols into the enactive, the iconic, and the symbolic, since the latter two categories seem to me ill-defined and ill-motivated. A classification of symbols as enactive, visual, auditory, etc., may be useful for some purposes of developmental psychology; but for our purposes here these distinctions cut across what seem to me more consequential differences among modes of reference.

[15] He understands very clearly and takes full advantage of the uses of muscular movements as elements of teachable symbol systems implementing the comprehension and retention of music. See especially *The Eurhythmics of Jaques-Dalcroze* (Boston, Small, Maynard, & Co., 1918), articles by P. B. Ingham (pp. 43–53) and E. Ingham (pp. 54–60).

ladder-climbings and window-washings by what he does. His miming may indeed exemplify activities involved in climbing or window-washing, as a picture may exemplify the color of a house it represents; but the picture is not a house, and the miming is not a climbing. The mime's walks, of course, may exemplify walking as well as denoting walks, just as "short" exemplifies shortness as well as denoting short words; but such self-denoting and self-exemplifying symbols are in the minority in pantomime as in English and in painting. The word "bird" or a picture of a bird, not being itself a bird, exemplifies no label denoting all and only birds; and a miming of a flight, not being a flight, exemplifies no label denoting all and only flights. A word or picture or pantomime does not often exemplify any label coextensive with it.

Some elements of the dance are primarily denotative, versions of the descriptive gestures of daily life (e.g., bowings, beckonings) or of ritual (e.g., signs of benediction, Hindu hand-postures).[16] But other movements, especially in the modern dance, primarily exemplify rather than denote. What they exemplify, however, are not standard or familiar activities, but rather rhythms and dynamic shapes. The exemplified patterns and properties may

---

[16] The dancer's act of benediction, like its replicas on the stage and in the church, denotes what is blessed. That the addressee of the dancer's gesture is not thereby among the blessed means only that the dancer, like the novelist, is making fictive use of a denoting symbol. But of course a gesture may, like the word "centaur", be denotative in character even though it denotes nothing. See further the last two paragraphs of this section.

reorganize experience, relating actions not usually associated or distinguishing others not usually differentiated, thus enriching allusion or sharpening discrimination. To regard these movements as illustrating verbal descriptions would of course be absurd; seldom can the just wording be found.[17] Rather, the label a movement exemplifies may be itself; such a movement, having no antecedent denotation, takes on the duties of a label denoting certain actions including itself. Here, as often elsewhere in the arts, the vocabulary evolves along with what it is used to convey.

Although exemplification is reference running from denotatum back to label, by no means every case of reference is a case of denotation or exemplification. An element may come to serve as a symbol for an element related to it in almost any way. Sometimes the underlying relationship is not referential, as when the symbol is the cause or effect of (and so sometimes called the sign of), or is just to the left of, or is similar to, what it denotes. In other cases reference runs along a chain of relationships, some or all of them referential. Thus one of two things may refer to the other via predicates exemplified; or one of two predicates refer to the other via things denoted. Some familiar types of symbolization can be distinguished in terms of such underlying relationships or chains; but no nonreferential relationship, and no chain, even (since reference is nontransitive) where each element refers to the next, is sufficient by itself to establish reference by its first element to

[17] See further VI,2.

II,4

its last. Each or either or neither of the two may refer to the other. And of course an element may symbolize another in more than one way.

Throughout most of this section, I have been contrasting exemplification with other relations, especially with possession (which is not reference at all) and with denotation (which runs in the opposite direction). But the contrasts must not be overdrawn. That a swatch exemplifies texture but not shape, or that a given picture exemplifies summer greenness but not newness, will usually be plain enough; but just which among its properties a thing exemplifies can often be hard to tell. Also, we have already seen that in some cases reference cannot be identified as denotation or exemplification, that in others the identification is arbitrary, and that in others a symbol and a predicate it exemplifies may be coextensive. Furthermore, label and sample are closer kin when the label denotes nothing; for fictive description and fictive representation reduce to exemplification of a special kind. "Centaur" or a picture of a centaur exemplifies being a centaur-description or a centaur-picture, or more generally, being a centaur-label. A picture of a green goblin, of course, need no more be green than be a goblin; it may be black and white but is, and exemplifies being, a green-goblin-picture. Description-as and representation-as, though pertaining to labels, are likewise matters of exemplification rather than of denotation.

Mention of fictive denotation raises the question whether we face a parallel problem of fictive exemplification. To say that a given phrase describes or a given picture represents Pickwick but not Don Quixote is to say, as we saw earlier,[18] that it is—and even exemplifies—being a Pickwick-label but not being a Don-Quixote-label. To say that Pickwick but not Don Quixote exemplifies clownishness is to say that "Pickwick" but not "Don Quixote" exemplifies (i.e., is denoted by and refers to) some label coextensive with "clown-label". But the two cases are not quite parallel; for in the first, a typical case of fictive denotation, what is purportedly *referred to* is fictive, while in the second what purportedly *refers* is fictive. Though we often ostensibly apply actual labels to fictive things, we can hardly apply fictive labels; for a label used exists. A thing may indeed exemplify a color-label that is not among the usual color-words or even not verbal at all; but to say that a thing h exemplifies its utterly nameless color is to say that the color of h, which is obviously named by "the color of h", is nameless. And to say that k exemplifies the nameless one among its several colors, that it exemplifies "has the nameless color exemplified by k", is to name what is described as nameless.

If a 'fictive' predicate is, rather, an actual predicate with null extension, and so not actually exemplified by anything, still it may be fictively exemplified; "winged horse" is exemplified by Pegasus in the sense that "Pegasus" exemplifies "winged-horse-label". Moreover, an empty as well as a non-empty predicate may be metaphorically exemplified; "angel" as well as "eagle" may be so exemplified by an aviator. But we have yet to consider the nature of metaphorical possession and exemplification.

---

[18] See I,5 and notes, above.

5. Facts and Figures

The picture is literally gray but only metaphorically sad. But is it literally or metaphorically cold in color? Am I saying metaphorically that it (or its color) is cold to the touch? Or am I using "cold" as I use "gray", to assign the picture to a certain class of colored objects? Isn't "cold" about as straightforward a way of indicating a range of color as is "gray" or "brownish" or "pure" or "bright"? If "cold" here is metaphorical, is speaking of colors as tones also metaphorical? And in speaking of a high note am I using a metaphor or only indicating relative position in the scale of pitch?

The usual (and metaphorical) answer is that a term like "cold color" or "high note" is a frozen metaphor—though it differs from a fresh one in age rather than temperature. A frozen metaphor has lost the vigor of youth, but remains a metaphor. Strangely, though, with progressive loss of its virility as a figure of speech, a metaphor becomes not less but more like literal truth. What vanishes is not its veracity but its vivacity. Metaphors, like new styles of representation, become more literal as their novelty wanes.

Is a metaphor, then, simply a juvenile fact, and a fact simply a senile metaphor? That needs some modification but does argue against excluding the metaphorical from the actual. Metaphorical possession is indeed not *literal* possession; but possession is actual whether metaphorical or literal. The metaphorical and the literal have to be distinguished within the actual. Calling a picture sad and calling it gray are simply different ways of classifying it. That is, although a predicate that applies to an object metaphorically does not apply literally, it nevertheless applies. Whether the application is metaphorical or literal depends upon some such feature as its novelty.

Mere novelty, however, does not quite make the difference. Every application of a predicate to a new event or a new-found object is new; but such routine projection [19] does not constitute metaphor. And even the earliest applications of a coined term need not be in the least metaphorical. Metaphor, it seems, is a matter of teaching an old word new tricks—of applying an old label in a new way. But what is the difference between merely applying a familiar label to new things and applying it in a novel way? Briefly, a metaphor is an affair between a predicate with a past and an object that yields while protesting. In routine projection, habit applies a label to a case not already decided. Arbitrary application of a newly coined term is equally unobstructed by prior decision. But metaphorical application of a label to an object defies an explicit or tacit prior denial of that label to that object. Where there is metaphor, there is conflict: the picture is sad rather than gay even though it is insentient and hence neither sad nor gay. Application of a term is metaphorical only if to some extent contra-indicated.

This, however, does not distinguish metaphorical truth from simple falsehood. Metaphor requires attraction as well as resistance—indeed, an attraction that overcomes

[19] On projection and projectibility, see *FFF*, esp. pp. 57–58, 81–83, 84–99.

resistance. To say that our picture is yellow is not metaphorical but merely false. To say that it is gay is false both literally and metaphorically. But to say that it is sad is metaphorically true even though literally false. Just as the picture clearly belongs under the label "gray" rather than under the label "yellow", it also clearly belongs under "sad" rather than under "gay". Conflict arises because the picture's being insentient implies that it is neither sad nor gay. Nothing can be both sad and not sad unless "sad" has two different ranges of application. If the picture is (literally) not sad and yet is (metaphorically) sad,[20] "sad" is used first as a label for certain sentient things or events, and then for certain insentient ones. To ascribe the predicate to something within either range is to make a statement that is true either literally or metaphorically. To ascribe the predicate to something in neither range (I leave other ranges of metaphorical application out of account for the moment) is to make a statement that is false both literally and metaphorically. Whereas falsity depends upon misassignment of a label, metaphorical truth depends upon reassignment.

Still, metaphor is not sheer ambiguity. Applying the term "cape" to a body of land on one occasion and to an article of clothing on another is using it with different and indeed mutually exclusive ranges but is not in either case

---

[20] Of course, where "sad" applies metaphorically, "metaphorically sad" applies literally; but this tells little about what constitutes being metaphorically sad.

metaphorical. How, then, do metaphor and ambiguity differ? Chiefly, I think, in that the several uses of a merely ambiguous term are coeval and independent; none either springs from or is guided by another. In metaphor, on the other hand, a term with an extension established by habit is applied elsewhere under the influence of that habit; there is both departure from and deference to precedent. When one use of a term precedes and informs another, the second is the metaphorical one. As time goes on, the history may fade and the two uses tend to achieve equality and independence; the metaphor freezes, or rather evaporates, and the residue is a pair of literal uses—mere ambiguity instead of metaphor.[21]

6. Schemata

An understanding of metaphor further requires the recognition that a label functions not in isolation but as belonging to a family. We categorize by sets of alternatives. Even constancy of literal application is usually relative to a set of labels: what counts as red, for example, will vary

[21] The treatment of metaphor in the following pages agrees in many matters with the excellent article by Max Black, "Metaphor", *Proceedings of the Aristotelian Society*, vol. 55 (1954), pp. 273–294, reprinted in his *Models and Metaphors* (Ithaca, N.Y., Cornell University Press, 1962), pp. 25–47. See also the well-known treatments by I. A. Richards, *The Philosophy of Rhetoric* (London, Oxford University Press, 1936), pp. 89–183, and by C. M. Turbayne, *The Myth of Metaphor* (New Haven, Yale University Press, 1962), pp. 11–27.

somewhat depending upon whether objects are being classified as red or nonred, or as red or orange or yellow or
green or blue or violet. What the admitted alternatives
are is of course less often determined by declaration than
by custom and context. Talk of schemata, categories, and
systems of concepts comes down in the end, I think, to
talk of such sets of labels.

The aggregate of the ranges of extension of the labels in a
schema may be called a *realm*. It consists of the objects
sorted by the schema—that is, of the objects denoted by at
least one of the alternative labels. Thus the range of "red"
comprises all red things while the realm in question may
comprise all colored things. But since the realm depends
upon the schema within which a label is functioning, and
since a label may belong to any number of such schemata,
even a label with a unique range seldom operates in a
unique realm.

Now metaphor typically involves a change not merely
of range but also of realm. A label along with others constituting a schema is in effect detached from the home realm
of that schema and applied for the sorting and organizing
of an alien realm. Partly by thus carrying with it a reorientation of a whole network of labels does a metaphor
give clues for its own development and elaboration. The
native and foreign realms may be sense-realms; or may be
wider, as when a poem is said to be touching, or an instrument to be sensitive; or narrower, as when different patterns of black and white are said to be of different hues; or
have nothing to do with sense-realms.

The shifts in range that occur in metaphor, then, usually amount to no mere distribution of family goods but to an expedition abroad. A whole set of alternative labels,[22] a whole apparatus of organization, takes over new territory. What occurs is a transfer of a schema, a migration of concepts, an alienation of categories. Indeed, a metaphor might be regarded as a calculated category-mistake [23]—or rather as a happy and revitalizing, even if bigamous, second marriage.

The alternatives of a schema need not be mutually exclusive; for instance, a set of color-terms with some of their ranges overlapping and some included in others will serve. Again, a schema is normally a linear or more complex array of labels; and the ordering—whether traditional as in the alphabet, syntactic as in a dictionary, or semantic as with color-names—and other relationships may be transferred. Moreover, the labels may themselves be predicates with two or more places; and such relative terms are no less amenable than categorical ones to metaphorical use. Just as "heavy" may apply metaphorically to a sound, so "heavier than" may apply metaphorically between one

[22] The implicit set of alternatives—the schema—may consist of two or many labels, and varies widely with context. To say that an idea is green is to contrast it not with ideas having other colors but with ideas having greater ripeness; and to say that an employee is green is simply to contrast him with others who are not green.

[23] On the notion of a category-mistake, see Gilbert Ryle, *The Concept of Mind* (London, Hutchinson's University Library, and New York, Barnes and Noble, Inc., 1949), pp. 16ff.

sound and another. A schema for sorting pairs of, and ordering, material objects is here applied for sorting pairs of, and ordering, sounds.

In all this, the aptness of an emphasis upon labels, of a nominalistic but not necessarily verbalistic orientation, becomes acutely apparent once more. Whatever reverence may be felt for classes or attributes, surely classes are not moved from realm to realm, nor are attributes somehow extracted from some objects and injected into others. Rather a set of terms, of alternative labels, is transported; and the organization they effect in the alien realm is guided by their habitual use in the home realm.

7. Transfer

A schema may be transported almost anywhere. The choice of territory for invasion is arbitrary; but the operation within that territory is almost never completely so. We may at will apply temperature-predicates to sounds or hues or personalities or to degrees of nearness to a correct answer; but *which* elements in the chosen realm are warm, or are warmer than others, is then very largely determinate. Even where a schema is imposed upon a most unlikely and uncongenial realm, antecedent practice channels the application of the labels. When a label has not only literal but prior metaphorical uses, these too may serve as part of the precedent for a later metaphorical application; perhaps, for instance, the way we apply "high" to sounds was guided by the earlier metaphorical application to numbers (via number of vibrations per second) rather than directly by the literal application according to altitude.[24]

Operant precedent does not, however, always consist solely of the way a label has been applied. What the label *exemplifies* may also be a powerful factor. This is most striking in the much discussed dichotomy of a miscellany under such a pair of nonsense syllables as "ping" and "pong".[25] The application of these words looks back not to how they have been used to classify anything but to how they have themselves been classified—not to what they antecedently denote but to what they antecedently exemplify. We apply "ping" to quick, light, sharp things, and "pong" to slow, heavy, dull things because "ping" and "pong" exemplify these properties. In our discussion of self-denoting terms, we have already noticed this phenomenon of samples taking over the denotation of terms they exemplify. Often a simple sample replaces a complex mixture of predicates, some literally and some metaphorically exemplified. Where the new labels had no prior denotation,[26] such supplantation does not constitute metaphor under the definition given; for rather than a label changing its extension, an extension here changes its label, and with respect to that extension the new label will be

[24] Or perhaps the metaphorical application to sounds preceded and guided later metaphorical application to numbers. My point does not depend upon the correctness of my etymology.

[25] See Gombrich, *Art and Illusion* (cited in I, note 5), p. 370.

[26] Having an established null denotation is quite a different matter from not having any established denotation. The extension of such terms as "centaur" and "Don Quixote" is null; and these terms, like terms with non-empty extensions, become metaphorical upon transfer.

only as metaphorical as the old. But when a label already has its own denotation and in replacing what it exemplifies usurps another, the new application is metaphorical.

The mechanism of transfer is often much less transparent. Why does "sad" apply to certain pictures and "gay" to others? What is meant by saying that a metaphorical application is 'guided by' or 'patterned after' the literal one? Sometimes we can contrive a plausible history: warm colors are those of fire, cold colors those of ice. In other cases, we have only fanciful alternative legends. Did numbers come to be higher and lower because piles grow higher as more stones are put on (despite the fact that holes go lower as more shovelfuls are taken out)? Or were numerals inscribed on tree trunks from the ground upward? Whatever the answer, these are all isolated questions of etymology. Presumably, we are being asked, rather, for some general account of how metaphorical use of a label reflects its literal use. On this there has been some suggestive speculation. Current literal use of many a term has been specialized from an initial, much broader application. The infant at first applies "mama" to almost anyone, learning only gradually to make important distinctions and restrict the range of the term. What seems a new use of a term may then consist of reapplying it over a region earlier vacated; and the way a term or schema applies there may depend upon half-conscious recollection of its earlier incarnation.[27] Personification

---

[27] The idea invites elaboration: the metaphorical application might with much use become literal also, with ambiguity thus resulting; and the two literal ranges might ultimately be reunited into the original one.

may thus echo aboriginal animism. The reapplication is nevertheless metaphorical; for what is literal is set by present practice rather than by ancient history. The home realm of a schema is the country of naturalization rather than of birth; and the returning expatriate is an alien despite his quickening memories. Explanation of metaphors along these lines has been provocatively set forth by Cassirer and others.[28] But however illuminating it may be, and however true for some cases, it obviously does not explain the metaphorical applications of all or even most terms. Only rarely can the adult adventures of a label be thus traced back to childhood deprivations.

The general question remains: what does a metaphor say and what makes it true? Is saying that a picture is sad saying elliptically that it is like a sad person? Metaphor has often been so construed as elliptical simile, and metaphorical truth as simply the literal truth of the expanded statement. But the simile cannot amount merely to saying that the picture is like the person in some respect or other; anything is like anything else to that extent. What the simile says in effect is that person and picture are alike in being sad, the one literally and the other metaphorically. Instead of metaphor reducing to simile, simile reduces to metaphor; or rather, the difference between simile and

---

[28] See Ernst Cassirer, *The Philosophy of Symbolic Forms* (original German edition, 1925), trans. Ralph Manheim (New Haven, Yale University Press, 1955), vol. II, pp. 36–43; Cassirer's *Language and Myth*, trans. S. K. Langer (New York and London, Harper Brothers, 1946), pp. 12, 23–39; and Owen Barfield, *Poetic Diction* (London, Faber and Faber, 1928), pp. 80–81.

metaphor is negligible.[29] Whether the locution be "is like" or "is", the figure *likens* picture to person by picking out a certain common feature: that the predicate "sad" applies to both, albeit to the person initially and to the picture derivatively.

If we are pressed to say what sort of similarity must obtain between what a predicate applies to literally and what it applies to metaphorically, we might ask in return what sort of similarity must obtain among the things a predicate applies to literally. How must past and future things be alike for a given predicate, say "green", to apply literally to them all? Having some property or other in common is not enough; they must have a *certain* property in common. But what property? Obviously the property named by the predicate in question; that is, the predicate must apply to all the things it must apply to. The question why predicates apply as they do metaphorically is much the same as the question why they apply as they do literally. And if we have no good answer in either case, perhaps that is because there is no real question. At any rate, the general explanation why things have the properties, literal and metaphorical, that they do have—why things are as they are—is a task I am content to leave to the cosmologist.

[29] Max Black makes this point clearly and forcefully in his article on metaphor; see his *Models and Metaphors*, p. 37: "It would be more illuminating in some of these cases to say that the metaphor creates the similarity than to say that it formulates some similarity antecedently existing."

Standards of truth are much the same whether the schema used is transferred or not. In either case, application of a term is fallible and thus subject to correction. We may make mistakes in applying either "red" or "sad" to colored objects; and we may bring tests of all sorts to bear upon our initial judgments: we may look again, compare, examine attendant circumstances, watch for corroborating and for conflicting judgments. Neither the status of initial credibility nor the process of verification by maximizing total credibility over all our judgments [30] is different in the two cases. Of course, a metaphorical sorting under a given schema is, since more novel, often less sharp and stable than the correlated literal sorting; but this is only a difference of degree. The literal as well as the metaphorical may be afflicted by vagueness and vacillation of all kinds; and literal applications of some schemata are, because of the delicacy or the unclarity of the distinctions called for, much less crisp and constant than some metaphorical applications of others. Difficulties in determining truth are by no means peculiar to metaphor.

Truth of a metaphor does not, indeed, guarantee its effectiveness. As there are irrelevant, tepid, and trivial literal truths, there are farfetched, feeble, and moribund metaphors. Metaphorical force requires a combination of novelty with fitness, of the odd with the obvious. The good metaphor satisfies while it startles. Metaphor is most

---

[30] Concerning this general matter, see my "Sense and Certainty", *Philosophical Review*, vol. 61 (1952), pp. 160–167.

potent when the transferred schema effects a new and notable organization rather than a mere relabeling of an old one. Where the organization by an immigrant schema coincides with an organization already otherwise effected in the new realm, the sole interest of the metaphor lies in how this organization is thus related to the application of the schema in its home realm, and sometimes to what the labels of the schema exemplify. But where an unaccustomed organization results, new associations and discriminations are also made within the realm of transfer; and the metaphor is the more telling as these are the more intriguing and significant. Since metaphor depends upon such transient factors as novelty and interest, its mortality is understandable. With repetition, a transferred application of a schema becomes routine, and no longer requires or makes any allusion to its base application. What was novel becomes commonplace, its past is forgotten, and metaphor fades to mere truth.

Metaphor permeates all discourse, ordinary and special, and we should have a hard time finding a purely literal paragraph anywhere. In that last prosaic enough sentence, I count five sure or possible—even if tired—metaphors. This incessant use of metaphor springs not merely from love of literary color but also from urgent need of economy. If we could not readily transfer schemata to make new sortings and orderings, we should have to burden ourselves with unmanageably many different schemata, either by adoption of a vast vocabulary of elementary terms or by prodigious elaboration of composite ones.

8. Modes of Metaphor

Metaphor comes in many varieties, most of them listed in the prodigious if chaotic standard catalogue of figures of speech. Some of these figures, of course, do not qualify as metaphors. Alliteration and apostrophe are purely syntactic, involving no transfer; and onomatopoeia consists merely of using a self-denoting label of a certain kind. Whether a euphemism is a metaphor or not depends upon whether it applies labels for proper things to improper things or only substitutes proper for improper labels.

Among metaphors some involve transfer of a schema between disjoint realms. In personification, labels are transferred from persons to things; in synecdoche, between a realm of wholes or classes and a realm of their proper parts or subclasses [31]; in antonomasia between things and their properties or labels.

But not for all metaphors are the two realms disjoint; sometimes one realm intersects or is an expansion or a contraction of the other. (See Figure 2.) In hyperbole, for instance, an ordered schema is in effect displaced downward. The large olive becomes supercolossal and the small one large; labels at the lower end of the schema (e.g., "small") are unused, and things at the upper end of the realm (the exceptionally large olive) are unlabeled in this application of the schema—unless the schema is extended,

---

[31] A realm of wholes is of course disjoint from a realm of their proper parts, and a realm of classes from a realm of their proper subclasses.

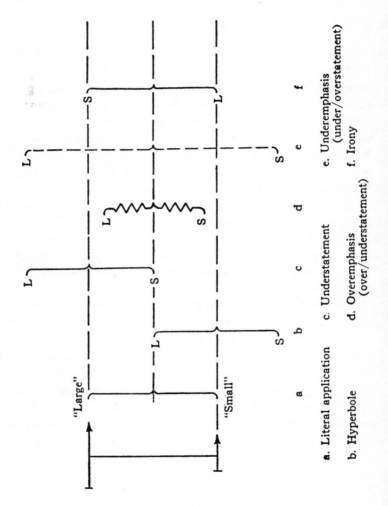

Figure 2

say by iteration of the prefix "super". In litotes, or understatement, exactly the opposite occurs. A superb performance becomes pretty fair and a good one passable; the top labels go unused and the bottom of the realm is undescribed. Hyperbole or understatement may be, so to speak, double-ended, with the entire schema squeezed into a central part of the original realm (leaving no labels for the extremes), or with a central part of the schema stretched out to cover the whole original realm (leaving nothing for the end labels to denote).

Although metaphor always involves transfer in the sense that some labels of the schema are given new extensions, the realm itself may remain constant under the transfer. In irony, for example, a schema is simply turned end for end and applied to its own realm in the opposite direction. What results is not a re-sorting but a reorientation. A misfortune becomes 'a fine thing' and a windfall 'tough luck'. In other cases a schema may return to its home realm by a longer route. Consider, for example, the metaphorical application of "blue" to pictures. Since "blue" also has a literal application to pictures, the metaphorical and literal applications are to the same territory. What has happened here is transfer from realm to realm and back again. A schema of color-predicates is carried first over to feelings and then back to colored objects. Its travels result in some displacement on its return (otherwise we shouldn't even know it had been away); but the displacement is far from total: a metaphorically blue picture is more likely to be literally blue than literally red. Sometimes a schema may take a longer round trip, with more stopovers, and be more drastically displaced on its return.

Two or more types of transfer are sometimes combined, as when an unreliable machine is called a true friend. Other metaphors are curbed or modified. Calling a picture brutal in coloring is not calling it brutal; the way is left open for calling the picture gentle in other respects, say in drawing, or even as a whole. "Brutal in coloring", since it has no different prior denotation, applies literally rather than metaphorically to the picture. It is a coloring-description in that although it may denote objects that differ in specific coloring it does not distinguish among objects of the same specific coloring. Yet clearly a metaphor is involved. In effect, the term "brutal" is metaphorically applied to the picture with respect to the coloring alone. In such a modified metaphor, a schema is, so to speak, transferred under explicit or tacit restrictions; its sorting of a realm must not cut across certain groupings already made there. Given free rein, the "brutal"-"gentle" schema sorts objects in one way; transferred under orders to effect a sorting based on coloring or based on pattern, the same schema sorts objects in other ways. Traveling under various instructions or along various routes, a given schema may have several different metaphorical applications in one realm.

Nonverbal as well as verbal labels may, of course, be applied metaphorically, say in a cartoon of a politician as a parrot, or of a despot as a dragon. And a blue painting of a trombone player involves complex, if unsubtle, transfer.

So much for metaphorical denotation. Metaphorical possession and exemplification are likewise parallel to their literal counterparts; and what was said earlier (section 3) about predicates and properties applies here as well. A picture is metaphorically sad if some label—verbal or not—that is coextensive with (i.e., has the same literal denotation as) "sad" metaphorically denotes the picture. The picture metaphorically exemplifies "sad" if "sad" is referred to by and metaphorically denotes the picture. And the picture metaphorically exemplifies sadness if some label coextensive with "sad" is referred to by and metaphorically denotes the picture. Since, as we have seen, the features that distinguish the metaphorical from the literal are transient, I shall often use "possession" and "exemplification" to cover both literal and metaphorical cases.

9. Expression

What is expressed is metaphorically exemplified. What expresses sadness is metaphorically sad. And what is metaphorically sad is actually but not literally sad, i.e., comes under a transferred application of some label coextensive with "sad".

Thus what is expressed is possessed, and what a face or picture expresses need not (but may) be emotions or ideas the actor or artist has, or those he wants to convey, or thoughts or feelings of the viewer or of a person depicted, or properties of anything else related in some other way to the symbol. Of course, a symbol is often said to express a property related to it in one of these ways, but I reserve the term "expression" to distinguish the central case where the property belongs to the symbol itself—regardless of cause or effect or intent or subject-matter. That the actor was despondent, the artist high, the spectator gloomy or nostalgic or euphoric, the subject inanimate, does not determine whether the face or picture is sad or not. The cheering face of the hypocrite expresses solicitude; and the stolid painter's picture of boulders may express agitation. The properties a symbol expresses are its own property.

But they are acquired property. They are not the homely features by which the objects and events that serve as symbols are classified literally, but are metaphorical imports. Pictures express sounds or feelings rather than colors. And the metaphorical transfer involved in expression is usually from or via an exterior realm rather than the interior transfer effected in hyperbole or litotes or irony. A pretentious picture does not express the modesty that may be sarcastically ascribed to it.

Properties expressed are, furthermore, not only metaphorically possessed but also referred to, exhibited, typified, shown forth. A square swatch does not usually exemplify squareness, and a picture that rapidly increases in market value does not express the property of being a gold mine. Normally, a swatch exemplifies only sartorial properties while a picture literally exemplifies only pictorial properties and metaphorically exemplifies only properties that are constant relative to pictorial properties.[32] And a

[32] A property is thus constant only if, although it may or may not remain constant where the pictorial properties vary, it never varies where the pictorial properties remain constant. In other words, if it occurs anywhere, it also occurs whenever the pictorial properties are the same. The constancy here in question obtains between the metaphorical extension of the expressed property and the literal extension of the basic pictorial properties; but a property thus constant also itself qualifies as a pictorial property. For a discussion of pictorial properties, see I,9, above.

picture expresses only properties—unlike that of being a gold mine—that it thus metaphorically exemplifies as a pictorial symbol. Daumier's *Laundress* so exemplifies and expresses weight but not any metaphorical property dependent upon the physical weight of the picture. In general, a symbol of a given kind—pictorial, musical, verbal, etc.—expresses only properties that it metaphorically exemplifies as a symbol of that kind.

Plainly, then, not every metaphorical statement about a symbol tells us what is expressed. Sometimes the metaphorical term is incorporated in a predicate that applies *literally* to the symbol, as in the modified metaphors noticed earlier or in the statement that a picture is by a painter in his cups. Sometimes the metaphorical property ascribed is possessed but not exemplified by the symbol or not constant relative to the required properties. And sometimes the metaphorical transfer involved is of the wrong kind. Only properties of the appropriate kind, metaphorically exemplified in the appropriate way, are expressed.

Though accuracy would often call for speaking of expression of predicates, I defer to a prissy prejudice by speaking throughout this section of expression of properties.[33] Yet by explaining expression in terms of the metaphorical exemplification of labels, I have risked the charge of making what a symbol expresses depend upon what is said about it—of leaving what a picture, for example, expresses to the accident of what terms happen to be used in

[33] No difficulty or obscurity is removed by such pussyfooting; and the bolder course of defying prejudice and speaking forthrightly of expression of labels rather than properties is surely to be recommended.

describing the picture, and hence of crediting the expression achieved not to the artist but to the commentator. This, of course, is a misunderstanding. A symbol must have every property it expresses; what counts is not whether anyone calls the picture sad but whether the picture is sad, whether the label "sad" does in fact apply. "Sad" may apply to a picture even though no one ever happens to use the term in describing the picture; and calling a picture sad by no means makes it so. This is not to say that whether a picture is sad is independent of the use of "sad" but that given, by practice or precept, the use of "sad", applicability to the picture is not arbitrary. Since practice and precept vary, possession and exemplification are not absolute either; and what is actually said about a picture is not always altogether irrelevant to what the picture expresses. Among the countless properties, most of them usually ignored, that a picture possesses, it expresses only those metaphorical properties it refers to. Establishment of the referential relationship is a matter of singling out certain properties for attention, of selecting associations with certain other objects. Verbal discourse is not least among the many factors that aid in founding and nurturing such associations. If nothing more than selection takes place here, still selection from such a multitude of eligibles amounts, as observed earlier, to virtual constitution. Pictures are no more immune than the rest of the world to the formative force of language even though they themselves, as symbols, also exert such a force upon the world, including language. Talking does not make the world or even pictures, but talking and pictures participate in making each other and the world as we know them.

Nonverbal as well as verbal labels may be metaphorically exemplified, and the corresponding properties expressed, by symbols of any kind. A picture of Churchill as a bulldog is metaphorical; and he may stand as a symbol that exemplifies the picture and expresses the bulldoggedness thus pictorially ascribed to him. We must note carefully that the pictorial metaphor here has to do not with what the picture may exemplify or express but with what may exemplify the picture and express the corresponding property.[34]

Expression, since limited to what is possessed and moreover to what has been acquired at second-hand, is doubly constrained as compared with denotation. Whereas almost anything can denote or even represent almost anything else, a thing can express only what belongs but did not originally belong to it. The difference between expression and literal exemplification, like the difference between more and less literal representation, is a matter of habit—a matter of fact rather than fiat.

Yet the habits differ widely with time and place and person and culture; and pictorial and musical expression are no less relative and variable than facial and gestural expression. Aldous Huxley, upon hearing some supposedly solemn music in India, wrote:

... I confess that, listen as I might, I was unable to hear anything particularly mournful or serious, anything spe-

---

[34] Or express the picture itself, if we stop pampering prejudice.

cially suggestive of self-sacrifice in the piece. To my Western ears it sounded much more cheerful than the dance which followed it.

Emotions are everywhere the same; but the artistic expression of them varies from age to age and from one country to another. We are brought up to accept the conventions current in the society into which we are born. This sort of art, we learn in childhood, is meant to excite laughter, that to evoke tears. Such conventions vary with great rapidity, even in the same country. There are Elizabethan dances that sound as melancholy to our ears as little funeral marches. Conversely, we are made to laugh by the "Anglo-Saxon attitudes" of the holiest personages in the drawings and miniatures of earlier centuries.[35]

The boundaries of expression, dependent upon the difference between exemplification and possession and also upon the difference between the metaphorical and the literal, are inevitably somewhat tenuous and transient. An Albers picture may pretty clearly *exemplify* certain shapes and colors and interrelations among them, while it merely possesses the property of being exactly 24½ inches high; but the distinction is not always so easily drawn. Again, the status of a property as metaphorical or literal is often unclear and seldom stable; for comparatively few properties are purely literal or permanently metaphorical. Even for very clear cases, ordinary discourse only sporadically observes the difference between expression and exemplification. Architects, for instance, like to speak of some buildings as expressing their functions. But however

[35] In "Music in India and Japan" (1926), reprinted in *On Art and Artists* (New York, Meridian Books, Inc., 1960), pp. 305–306.

effectively a glue factory may typify glue-making, it exemplifies being a glue factory literally rather than metaphorically. A building may express fluidity or frivolity or fervor [36]; but to express being a glue factory it would have to be something else, say a toothpick plant. But since reference to a possessed property is the common core of metaphorical and literal exemplification, and the distinction between these is ephemeral, popular use of the term "expression" for cases of both kinds is not very surprising or pernicious.

Music and dance alike may exemplify rhythmic patterns, for example, and express peace or pomp or passion; and music may express properties of movement while dance may express properties of sound. With respect to verbal symbols, ordinary usage is so undiscriminating that a word or passage may be said to express not only what the writer thought or felt or intended, or the effect upon the reader, or properties possessed by or ascribed to a subject, but even what is described or stated. In the special sense I have been discussing, though, a verbal symbol may express only properties it metaphorically exemplifies; naming a property and expressing it are different matters; and a poem or story need not express what it says or say what it expresses. A tale of fast action may be slow, a biography of a benefactor bitter, a description of colorful music

[36] A building may "express a mood—gaiety and movement in the whirly little Comedy Theatre, Berlin—or even ideas about astronomy and relativity like Mendlesohn's Einstein tower, or nationalism like some of Hitler's architecture", according to Richard Sheppard in "Monument to the Architect?", *The Listener*, June 8, 1967, p. 746.

drab, and a play about boredom electric. To describe, as to depict, a person as sad or as expressing sadness is not necessarily to express sadness; not every sad-person-description or -picture or every person-expressing-sadness-description or -picture is itself sad. And a passage or picture may exemplify or express without describing or representing, and even without being a description or representation at all— as in the case of some passages from James Joyce and some drawings by Kandinsky.[37]

Yet though exemplification and expression are distinct from, and run in the opposite direction from, representation and description, all are intimately related modes of symbolization. In these varied ways, a symbol may select from and organize its universe and be itself in turn informed or transformed. Representation and description relate a symbol to things it applies to. Exemplification relates the symbol to a label that denotes it, and hence indirectly to the things (including the symbol itself) in the range of that label. Expression relates the symbol to a label that metaphorically denotes it, and hence indirectly not only to the given metaphorical but also to the literal range of that label. And various longer chains of the elementary referential relationships of labels to things and other labels, and of things to labels, may run from any symbol.

---

[37] Kandinsky's caption for one of these is quoted at the beginning of the present chapter. Of course, it does not matter whether Kandinsky and the reader see ear to ear on this drawing; one may go "ping" when the other goes "pong".

EXPRESSION

To exemplify or express is to display rather than depict or describe; but as representation may be stereotyped or searching, and exemplification trite or telling, so may expression be platitudinous or provocative. A property expressed, though it must be constant relative to certain literal properties, need not coincide in extension with any easy and familiar literal description. Finding a disjunction of conjunctions of ordinary literal properties of pictures that is even approximately equivalent to metaphorical sadness would give us a good deal of trouble. The expressive symbol, with its metaphorical reach, not only partakes of the greenness of neighboring pastures and the exotic atmospheres of farther shores, but often in consequence uncovers unnoticed affinities and antipathies among symbols of its own kind. From the nature of metaphor derives some of the characteristic capacity of expression for suggestive allusion, elusive suggestion, and intrepid transcendence of basic boundaries.

Emphasis on the denotative (representative or descriptive), the exemplificatory ('formal' or 'decorative'), and the expressive in the arts varies with art, artist, and work. Sometimes one aspect dominates to the virtual exclusion of the other two; compare Debussy's *La Mer*, Bach's *Goldberg Variations*, and Charles Ives's *Fourth Symphony*, for instance; or a Dürer watercolor, a Jackson Pollock painting, and a Soulages lithograph. In other cases two or all three aspects, fused or in counterpoint, are almost equally prominent; in the film *Last Year at Marienbad*, the narrative thread, though never abandoned, is disrupted to let through insistent cadences and virtually indescribable sensory and emotional qualities. The choice is up to the artist, and judgment up to the critic. Nothing in the present analysis of symbolic functions offers any support for manifestos to the effect that representation is an indispensable requirement for art, or is an insuperable barrier to it, or that expression without representation is the highest achievement of the human spirit, or that representation and expression alike corrupt exemplification, or so on. If representation is reprehensible or revered, if expression is exalted or execrated, if exemplification is the essence of poverty or purity, this must be on other grounds.

Some writers, according to their temperament, have regarded expression either as sacredly occult or as hopelessly obscure. Perhaps the foregoing pages have exposed the main factors fostering such admiration or exasperation: first, the extreme ambiguities and inconstancies of ordinary usage; second, the great multiplicity of labels that apply to any object; third, the variation in application of a label with the set of alternatives in question; fourth, the different referents assigned the same schema under different symbolic systems; fifth, the variety of metaphorical applications that a schema with a single literal application may have to a single realm under different types and routes of transfer; and finally, the very novelty and instability that distinguishes metaphor. The first four of these troubles beset the literal as well as the metaphorical use of terms; and the last two are symptomatic neither of uncontrolled caprice nor of impenetrable mystery but of exploration and discovery. I hope that chaos has been reduced, if not to clarity, at least to lesser confusion.

In summary, if *a* expresses *b* then: (1) *a* possesses or is denoted by *b*; (2) this possession or denotation is metaphorical; and (3) *a* refers to *b*.

No test for detecting what a work expresses has been sought here; after all, a definition of hydrogen gives us no ready way of telling how much of the gas is in this room. Nor has any precise definition been offered for the elementary relation of expression we have been examining. Rather, it has been subsumed under metaphorical exemplification, and circumscribed somewhat more narrowly by some additional requirements, without any claim that these are sufficient.[38] The concern has been to compare and contrast this relation with such other major kinds of reference as exemplification, representation, and description. So far we have succeeded better with expression than with representation and description, which we have not yet been able to distinguish from one another.

In the next chapter, I want to make a fresh start, with a problem remote from those we have been discussing. Only much later will the course of our investigation make connection with what we have done so far.

[38] But some superficially odd cases meeting the stated requirements seem entitled to admission; many a work, I think, may quite appropriately be said to express eloquently its unintentional clumsiness or stupidity.

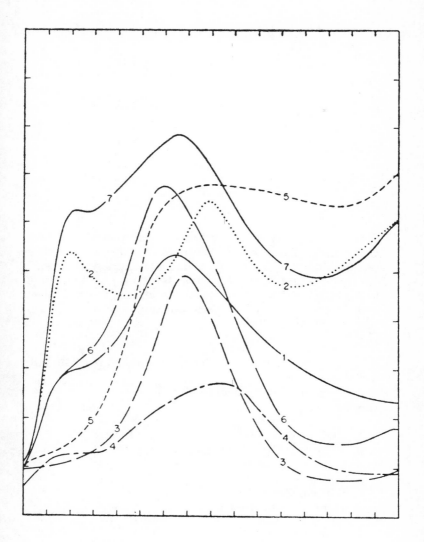

Reverse

Spectrographic study of various green pigments mixed with rutile TiO_2. From Ruth M. Johnston, "Spectrophotography for the Analysis and Description of Color", *Journal of Paint Technology*, vol. 39 (1967), p. 349, figure 9. Reproduced by permission of the author, the publisher, and the Pittsburgh Plate Glass Co.; and with the cooperation of Dr. R. L. Feller.

KEY

From left to right: wave length from 380 to 700 millimicrons.
From bottom to top: percent reflectance.
Curves:
1. Chrome Green
2. Chrome Oxide Green
3. Tungstate Green Toner
4. Pigment Green B
5. Green Gold
6. Phthalo Green
7. Hydrated Chrome Oxide

III

ART AND AUTHENTICITY

. . . the most tantalizing question of all: If a fake is so expert that even after the most thorough and trustworthy examination its authenticity is still open to doubt, is it or is it not as satisfactory a work of art as if it were unequivocally genuine?

Aline B. Saarinen*

1. The Perfect Fake

Forgeries of works of art present a nasty practical problem to the collector, the curator, and the art historian, who must often expend taxing amounts of time and energy in determining whether or not particular objects are genuine. But the theoretical problem raised is even more acute. The hardheaded question why there is any aesthetic difference between a deceptive forgery and an original work challenges a basic premiss on which the very functions of collector, museum, and art historian depend. A philosopher of art caught without an answer to this question is at least as badly off as a curator of paintings caught taking a Van Meegeren for a Vermeer.

The question is most strikingly illustrated by the case of a given work and a forgery or copy or reproduction of it. Suppose we have before us, on the left, Rembrandt's orig-

New York Times Book Review, July 30, 1961, p. 14.

inal painting *Lucretia* and, on the right, a superlative imitation of it. We know from a fully documented history that
the painting on the left is the original; and we know from
X-ray photographs and microscopic examination and
chemical analysis that the painting on the right is a recent
fake. Although there are many differences between the
two—e.g., in authorship, age, physical and chemical characteristics, and market value—we cannot see any difference between them; and if they are moved while we sleep,
we cannot then tell which is which by merely looking at
them. Now we are pressed with the question whether
there can be any aesthetic difference between the two
pictures; and the questioner's tone often intimates that the
answer is plainly *no*, that the only differences here are
aesthetically irrelevant.

We must begin by inquiring whether the distinction
between what can and what cannot be seen in the pictures
by 'merely looking at them' is entirely clear. We are looking at the pictures, but presumably not 'merely looking' at
them, when we examine them under a microscope or
fluoroscope. Does merely looking, then, mean looking
without the use of any instrument? This seems a little
unfair to the man who needs glasses to tell a painting from
a hippopotamus. But if glasses are permitted at all, how
strong may they be, and can we consistently exclude the
magnifying glass and the microscope? Again, if incandescent light is permitted, can violet-ray light be ruled out?
And even with incandescent light, must it be of medium
intensity and from a normal angle, or is a strong raking

light permitted? All these cases might be covered by saying that 'merely looking' is looking at the pictures without any use of instruments other than those customarily used in looking at things in general. This will cause trouble when we turn, say, to certain miniature illuminations or Assyrian cylinder seals that we can hardly distinguish from the crudest copies without using a strong glass. Furthermore, even in our case of the two pictures, subtle differences of drawing or painting discoverable only with a magnifying glass may still, quite obviously, be aesthetic differences between the pictures. If a powerful microscope is used instead, this is no longer the case; but just how much magnification is permitted? To specify what is meant by merely looking at the pictures is thus far from easy; but for the sake of argument,[1] let us suppose that all these difficulties have been resolved and the notion of 'merely looking' made clear enough.

Then we must ask who is assumed to be doing the looking. Our questioner does not, I take it, mean to suggest that there is no aesthetic difference between two pictures if at least one person, say a cross-eyed wrestler, can see no difference. The more pertinent question is whether there can be any aesthetic difference if nobody, not even the most skilled expert, can ever tell the pictures apart by merely looking at them. *But notice now that no one can*

---

[1] And only for the sake of argument—only in order not to obscure the central issue. All talk of mere looking in what follows is to be understood as occurring within the scope of this temporary concession, not as indicating any acceptance of the notion on my part.

ever ascertain by merely looking at the pictures that no one ever has been or will be able to tell them apart by merely looking at them. In other words, the question in its present form concedes that no one can ascertain by merely looking at the pictures that there is no aesthetic difference between them. This seems repugnant to our questioner's whole motivation. For if merely looking can never establish that two pictures are aesthetically the same, something that is beyond the reach of any given looking is admitted as constituting an aesthetic difference. And in that case, the reason for not admitting documents and the results of scientific tests becomes very obscure.

The real issue may be more accurately formulated as the question whether there is any aesthetic difference between the two pictures *for me* (or for *x*) if I (or *x*) cannot tell them apart by merely looking at them. But this is not quite right either. For I can never ascertain merely by looking at the pictures that even I shall never be able to see any difference between them. And to concede that something beyond any given looking at the pictures by me may constitute an aesthetic difference between them *for me* is, again, quite at odds with the tacit conviction or suspicion that activates the questioner.

Thus the critical question amounts finally to this: is there any aesthetic difference between the two pictures for *x* at *t*, where *t* is a suitable period of time, if *x* cannot tell them apart by merely looking at them at *t*? Or in other words, can anything that *x* does not discern by merely looking at the pictures at *t* constitute an aesthetic difference between them for *x* at *t*?

2. The Answer

In setting out to answer this question, we must bear clearly in mind that what one can distinguish at any given moment by merely looking depends not only upon native visual acuity but upon practice and training.[2] Americans look pretty much alike to a Chinese who has never looked at many of them. Twins may be indistinguishable to all but their closest relatives and acquaintances. Moreover, only through looking at them when someone has named them for us can we learn to tell Joe from Jim upon merely looking at them. Looking at people or things attentively, with the knowledge of certain presently invisible respects in which they differ, increases our ability to discriminate between them—and between other things or other people —upon merely looking at them. Thus pictures that look just alike to the newsboy come to look quite unlike to him by the time he has become a museum director.

Although I see no difference now between the two pic-

[2] Germans learning English often cannot, without repeated effort and concentrated attention, hear any difference at all between the vowel sounds in "cup" and "cop". Like effort may sometimes be needed by the native speaker of a language to discern differences in color, etc., that are not marked by his elementary vocabulary. Whether language affects actual sensory discrimination has long been debated among psychologists, anthropologists, and linguists; see the survey of experimentation and controversy in Segall, Campbell, and Herskovits, *The Influence of Culture on Visual Perception* (Indianapolis and New York, The Bobbs-Merrill Co., Inc., 1966), pp. 34–48. The issue is unlikely to be resolved without greater clarity in the use of "sensory", "perceptual", and "cognitive", and more care in distinguishing between what a person can do at a given time and what he can learn to do.

tures in question, I may learn to see a difference between them. I cannot determine now by merely looking at them, or in any other way, that I *shall* be able to learn. But the information that they are very different, that the one is the original and the other the forgery, argues against any inference to the conclusion that I *shall not* be able to learn. And the fact that I may later be able to make a perceptual distinction between the pictures that I cannot make now constitutes an aesthetic difference between them that is important to me now.

Furthermore, to look at the pictures now with the knowledge that the left one is the original and the other the forgery may help develop the ability to tell which is which later by merely looking at them. Thus, with information not derived from the present or any past looking at the pictures, the present looking may have a quite different bearing upon future lookings from what it would otherwise have. The way the pictures in fact differ constitutes an aesthetic difference between them for me now because my knowledge of the way they differ bears upon the role of the present looking in training my perceptions to discriminate between these pictures, and between others.

But that is not all. My knowledge of the difference between the two pictures, just because it affects the relationship of the present to future lookings, informs the very character of my present looking. This knowledge instructs me to look at the two pictures differently now, even if what I see is the same. Beyond testifying that I may learn to see a difference, it also indicates to some extent the kind of scrutiny to be applied now, the comparisons and contrasts to be made in imagination, and the relevant associations to be brought to bear. It thereby guides the selection, from my past experience, of items and aspects for use in my present looking. Thus not only later but right now, the unperceived difference between the two pictures is a consideration pertinent to my visual experience with them.

In short, although I cannot tell the pictures apart merely by looking at them now, the fact that the left-hand one is the original and the right-hand one a forgery constitutes an aesthetic difference between them for me now because knowledge of this fact (1) stands as evidence that there may be a difference between them that I can learn to perceive, (2) assigns the present looking a role as training toward such a perceptual discrimination, and (3) makes consequent demands that modify and differentiate my present experience in looking at the two pictures.[3]

Nothing depends here upon my ever actually perceiving or being able to perceive a difference between the two pictures. What informs the nature and use of my present visual experience is not the fact or the assurance that such a perceptual discrimination is within my reach, but evi-

---

[3] In saying that a difference *between the pictures* that is thus relevant to my present experience in looking at them constitutes an aesthetic difference between them, I am of course not saying that everything (e.g., drunkenness, snow blindness, twilight) that may cause my experiences of them to differ constitutes such an aesthetic difference. Not every difference in or arising from how the pictures happen to be looked at counts; only differences in or arising from how they are to be looked at. Concerning the aesthetic, more will be said later in this section and in VI,3–6.

dence that it may be; and such evidence is provided by the known factual differences between the pictures. Thus the pictures differ aesthetically for me now even if no one will ever be able to tell them apart merely by looking at them.

But suppose it could be *proved* that no one ever will be able to see any difference? This is about as reasonable as asking whether, if it can be proved that the market value and yield of a given U.S. bond and one of a certain nearly bankrupt company will always be the same, there is any financial difference between the two bonds. For what sort of proof could be given? One might suppose that if nobody—not even the most skilled expert—has ever been able to see any difference between the pictures, then the conclusion that I shall never be able to is quite safe; but, as in the case of the Van Meegeren forgeries[4] (of which, more later), distinctions not visible to the expert up to a given time may later become manifest even to the observant layman. Or one might think of some delicate scanning device that compares the color of two pictures at every point and registers the slightest discrepancy. What, though, is meant here by "at every point"? At no mathematical point, of course, is there any color at all; and even some physical particles are too small to have color. The scanning device must thus cover at each instant a region

[4] For a detailed and fully illustrated account, see P. B. Coremans, *Van Meegeren's Faked Vermeers and De Hooghs,* trans. A. Hardy and C. Hutt (Amsterdam, J. M. Meulenhoff, 1949). The story is outlined in Sepp Schüller, *Forgers, Dealers, Experts,* trans. J. Cleugh (New York, G. P. Putnam's Sons, 1960), pp. 95-105.

big enough to have color but at least as small as any perceptible region. Just how to manage this is puzzling since "perceptible" in the present context means "discernible by merely looking", and thus the line between perceptible and nonperceptible regions seems to depend on the arbitrary line between a magnifying glass and a microscope. If some such line is drawn, we can never be sure that the delicacy of our instruments is superior to the maximal attainable acuity of unaided perception. Indeed, some experimental psychologists are inclined to conclude that every measurable difference in light can sometimes be detected by the naked eye.[5] And there is a further difficulty. Our scanning device will examine color—that is, reflected light. Since reflected light depends partly upon incident light, illumination of every quality, of every intensity, and from every direction must be tried. And for each case, especially since the paintings do not have a plane surface, a complete scanning must be made from every angle. But of course we cannot cover every variation, or even determine a single absolute correspondence, in even one respect. Thus the search for a proof that I shall never be able to see any difference between the two pictures is futile for more than technological reasons.

---

[5] Not surprisingly, since a single quantum of light may excite a retinal receptor. See M. H. Pirenne and F. H. C. Marriott, "The Quantum Theory of Light and the Psycho-Physiology of Vision", in *Psychology*, ed. S. Koch (New York and London, McGraw-Hill Co., Inc., 1959), vol. I, p. 290; also Theodore C. Ruch, "Vision", in *Medical Psychology and Biophysics* (Philadelphia, W. B. Saunders Co., 1960), p. 426.

Yet suppose we are nevertheless pressed with the question whether, if proof *were* given, there would then be any aesthetic difference for me between the pictures. And suppose we answer this farfetched question in the negative. This will still give our questioner no comfort. For the net result would be that if no difference between the pictures can in fact be perceived, then the existence of an aesthetic difference between them will rest entirely upon what is or is not proved by means other than merely looking at them. This hardly supports the contention that there can be no aesthetic difference without a perceptual difference.

Returning from the realm of the ultra-hypothetical, we may be faced with the protest that the vast aesthetic difference thought to obtain between the Rembrandt and the forgery cannot be accounted for in terms of the search for, or even the discovery of, perceptual differences so slight that they can be made out, if at all, only after much experience and long practice. This objection can be dismissed at once; for minute perceptual differences can bear enormous weight. The clues that tell me whether I have caught the eye of someone across the room are almost indiscernible. The actual differences in sound that distinguish a fine from a mediocre performance can be picked out only by the well-trained ear. Extremely subtle changes can alter the whole design, feeling, or expression of a painting. Indeed, the slightest perceptual differences sometimes matter the most aesthetically; gross physical damage to a fresco may be less consequential than slight but smug retouching.

THE ANSWER

All I have attempted to show, of course, is that the two pictures can differ aesthetically, not that the original is better than the forgery. In our example, the original probably is much the better picture, since Rembrandt paintings are in general much better than copies by unknown painters. But a copy of a Lastman by Rembrandt may well be better than the original. We are not called upon here to make such particular comparative judgments or to formulate canons of aesthetic evaluation. We have fully met the demands of our problem by showing that the fact that we cannot tell our two pictures apart merely by looking at them does not imply that they are aesthetically the same—and thus does not force us to conclude that the forgery is as good as the original.

The example we have been using throughout illustrates a special case of a more general question concerning the aesthetic significance of authenticity. Quite aside from the occurrence of forged duplication, does it matter whether an original work is the product of one or another artist or school or period? Suppose that I can easily tell two pictures apart but cannot tell who painted either except by using some device like X-ray photography. Does the fact that the picture is or is not by Rembrandt make any aesthetic difference? What is involved here is the discrimination not of one picture from another but of the class of Rembrandt paintings from the class of other paintings. My chance of learning to make this discrimination correctly— of discovering projectible characteristics that differentiate Rembrandts in general from non-Rembrandts—depends heavily upon the set of examples available as a basis. Thus the fact that the given picture belongs to the one class or the other is important for me to know in learning how to tell Rembrandt paintings from others. In other words, my present (or future) inability to determine the authorship of the given picture without use of scientific apparatus does not imply that the authorship makes no aesthetic difference to me; for knowledge of the authorship, no matter how obtained, can contribute materially toward developing my ability to determine without such apparatus whether or not any picture, including this one on another occasion, is by Rembrandt.

Incidentally, one rather striking puzzle is readily solved in these terms. When Van Meegeren sold his pictures as Vermeers, he deceived most of the best-qualified experts; and only by his confession was the fraud revealed.[6] Nowadays even the fairly knowing layman is astonished that any competent judge could have taken a Van Meegeren for a Vermeer, so obvious are the differences. What has

[6] That the forgeries purported to have been painted during a period from which no Vermeers were known made detection more difficult but does not essentially alter the case. Some art historians, on the defensive for their profession, claim that the most perceptive critics suspected the forgeries very early; but actually some of the foremost recognized authorities were completely taken in and for some time even refused to believe Van Meegeren's confession. The reader has a more recent example now before him in the revelation that the famous bronze horse, long exhibited in the Metropolitan Museum and proclaimed as a masterpiece of classical Greek sculpture, is a modern forgery. An official of the museum noticed a seam that apparently neither he nor anyone else had ever seen before, and scientific testing followed. No expert has come forward to claim earlier doubts on aesthetic grounds.

happened? The general level of aesthetic sensibility has hardly risen so fast that the layman of today sees more acutely than the expert of twenty years ago. Rather, the better information now at hand makes the discrimination easier. Presented with a single unfamiliar picture at a time, the expert had to decide whether it was enough like known Vermeers to be by the same artist. And every time a Van Meegeren was added to the corpus of pictures accepted as Vermeers, the criteria for acceptance were modified thereby; and the mistaking of further Van Meegerens for Vermeers became inevitable. Now, however, not only have the Van Meegerens been subtracted from the precedent-class for Vermeer, but also a precedent-class for Van Meegeren has been established. With these two precedent-classes before us, the characteristic differences become so conspicuous that telling other Van Meegerens from Vermeers offers little difficulty. Yesterday's expert might well have avoided his errors if he had had a few known Van Meegerens handy for comparison. And to-day's layman who so cleverly spots a Van Meegeren may well be caught taking some quite inferior school-piece for a Vermeer.

In answering the questions raised above, I have not attempted the formidable task of defining "aesthetic" in general,[7] but have simply argued that since the exercise, training, and development of our powers of discriminating among works of art are plainly aesthetic activities, the aesthetic properties of a picture include not only those

[7] I shall come to that question much later, in Chapter VI.

found by looking at it but also those that determine how it is to be looked at. This rather obvious fact would hardly have needed underlining but for the prevalence of the time-honored Tingle-Immersion theory,[8] which tells us that the proper behavior on encountering a work of art is to strip ourselves of all the vestments of knowledge and experience (since they might blunt the immediacy of our enjoyment), then submerge ourselves completely and gauge the aesthetic potency of the work by the intensity and duration of the resulting tingle. The theory is absurd on the face of it and useless for dealing with any of the important problems of aesthetics; but it has become part of the fabric of our common nonsense.

3. The Unfakable

A second problem concerning authenticity is raised by the rather curious fact that in music, unlike painting, there is no such thing as a forgery of a known work. There are, indeed, compositions falsely purporting to be by Haydn as there are paintings falsely purporting to be by Rembrandt; but of the *London Symphony*, unlike the *Lucretia*, there can be no forgeries. Haydn's manuscript is no more genuine an instance of the score than is a printed copy off the press this morning, and last night's performance no less genuine than the premiere. Copies of the score may vary in accuracy, but all accurate copies, even if forgeries of Haydn's manuscript, are equally genuine instances of the

[8] Attributed to Immanuel Tingle and Joseph Immersion (*ca.* 1800).

score. Performances may vary in correctness and quality and even in 'authenticity' of a more esoteric kind; but all correct performances are equally genuine instances of the work.[9] In contrast, even the most exact copies of the Rembrandt painting are simply imitations or forgeries, not new instances, of the work. Why this difference between the two arts?

Let us speak of a work of art as *autographic* if and only if the distinction between original and forgery of it is significant; or better, if and only if even the most exact duplication of it does not thereby count as genuine.[10] If a work of art is autographic, we may also call that art autographic. Thus painting is autographic, music nonautographic, or *allographic*. These terms are introduced purely for convenience; nothing is implied concerning the relative individuality of expression demanded by or attainable in these arts. Now the problem before us is to account for the fact that some arts but not others are autographic.

One notable difference between painting and music is

[9] There may indeed be forgeries of performances. Such forgeries are performances that purport to be by a certain musician, etc; but these, if in accordance with the score, are nevertheless genuine instances of the work. And what concerns me here is a distinction among the arts that depends upon whether there can be forgeries of works, not upon whether there can be forgeries of instances of works. See further what is said in section 4 below concerning forgeries of editions of literary works and of musical performances.

[10] This is to be taken as a preliminary version of a difference we must seek to formulate more precisely. Much of what follows in this chapter has likewise the character of an exploratory introduction to matters calling for fuller and more detailed inquiry in later chapters.

that the composer's work is done when he has written the score, even though the performances are the end-products, while the painter has to finish the picture. No matter how many studies or revisions are made in either case, painting is in this sense a one-stage and music a two-stage art. Is an art autographic, then, if and only if it is one-stage? Counterexamples come readily to mind. In the first place, literature is not autographic though it is one-stage. There is no such thing as a forgery of Gray's *Elegy*. Any accurate copy of the text of a poem or novel is as much the original work as any other. Yet what the writer produces is ultimate; the text is not merely a means to oral readings as a score is a means to performances in music. An unrecited poem is not so forlorn as an unsung song; and most literary works are never read aloud at all. We might try to make literature into a two-stage art by considering the silent readings to be the end-products, or the instances of a work; but then the lookings at a picture and the listenings to a performance would qualify equally as end-products or instances, so that painting as well as literature would be two-stage and music three-stage. In the second place, printmaking is two-stage and yet autographic. The etcher, for example, makes a plate from which impressions are then taken on paper. These prints are the end-products; and although they may differ appreciably from one another, all are instances of the original work. But even the most exact copy produced otherwise than by printing from that plate counts not as an original but as an imitation or forgery.

114   III,3

So far, our results are negative: not all one-stage arts are autographic and not all autographic arts are one-stage. Furthermore, the example of printmaking refutes the unwary assumption that in every autographic art a particular work exists only as a unique object. The line between an autographic and an allographic art does not coincide with that between a singular and a multiple art. About the only positive conclusion we can draw here is that the autographic arts are those that are singular in the earliest stage; etching is singular in its first stage—the plate is unique—and painting in its only stage. But this hardly helps; for the problem of explaining why some arts are singular is much like the problem of explaining why they are autographic.

4. The Reason

Why, then, can I no more make a forgery of Haydn's symphony or of Gray's poem than I can make an original of Rembrandt's painting or of his etching *Tobit Blind*? Let us suppose that there are various handwritten copies and many editions of a given literary work. Differences between them in style and size of script or type, in color of ink, in kind of paper, in number and layout of pages, in condition, etc., do not matter. All that matters is what may be called *sameness of spelling*: exact correspondence as sequences of letters, spaces, and punctuation marks. Any sequence—even a forgery of the author's manuscript or of a given edition—that so corresponds to a correct copy is

III,4   115 itself correct, and nothing is more the original work than is such a correct copy. And since whatever is not an original of the work must fail to meet such an explicit standard of correctness, there can be no deceptive imitation, no forgery, of that work. To verify the spelling or to spell correctly is all that is required to identify an instance of the work or to produce a new instance. In effect, the fact that a literary work is in a definite notation, consisting of certain signs or characters that are to be combined by concatenation, provides the means for distinguishing the properties constitutive of the work from all contingent properties—that is, for fixing the required features and the limits of permissible variation in each. Merely by determining that the copy before us is spelled correctly we can determine that it meets all requirements for the work in question. In painting, on the contrary, with no such alphabet of characters, none of the pictorial properties—none of the properties the picture has as such—is distinguished as constitutive; no such feature can be dismissed as contingent, and no deviation as insignificant. The only way of ascertaining that the *Lucretia* before us is genuine is thus to establish the historical fact that it is the actual object made by Rembrandt. Accordingly, physical identification of the product of the artist's hand, and consequently the conception of forgery of a particular work, assume a significance in painting that they do not have in literature.[11]

[11] Such identification does not guarantee that the object possesses the pictorial properties it had originally. Rather, reliance on physical or historical identification is transcended only where we have means of ascertaining that the requisite properties are present.

THE REASON

What has been said of literary texts obviously applies also to musical scores. The alphabet is different; and the characters in a score, rather than being strung one after the other as in a text, are disposed in a more complex array. Nevertheless, we have a limited set of characters and of positions for them; and correct spelling, in only a slightly expanded sense, is still the sole requirement for a genuine instance of a work. Any false copy is wrongly spelled—has somewhere in place of the right character either another character or an illegible mark that is not a character of the notation in question at all.

But what of performances of music? Music is not autographic in this second stage either, yet a performance by no means consists of characters from an alphabet. Rather, the constitutive properties demanded of a performance of the symphony are those *prescribed in* the score; and performances that comply with the score may differ appreciably in such musical features as tempo, timbre, phrasing, and expressiveness. To determine compliance requires, indeed, something more than merely knowing the alphabet; it requires the ability to correlate appropriate sounds with the visible signs in the score—to recognize, so to speak, correct pronunciation though without necessarily understanding what is pronounced. The competence required to identify or produce sounds called for by a score increases with the complexity of the composition, but there is nevertheless a theoretically decisive test for compliance; and a performance, whatever its interpretative fidelity and independent merit, has or has not all the constitutive properties of a given work, and is or is not strictly a performance of that work, according as it does or does not pass this test. No historical information concerning the production of the performance can affect the result. Hence deception as to the facts of production is irrelevant, and the notion of a performance that is a forgery of the work is quite empty.

Yet there are forgeries of performances as there are of manuscripts and editions. What makes a performance an instance of a given work is not the same as what makes a performance a premiere, or played by a certain musician or upon a Stradivarius violin. Whether a performance has these latter properties is a matter of historical fact; and a performance falsely purporting to have any such property counts as a forgery, not of the musical composition but of a given performance or class of performances.

The comparison between printmaking and music is especially telling. We have already noted that etching, for example, is like music in having two stages and in being multiple in its second stage; but that whereas music is autographic in neither stage, printmaking is autographic in both. Now the situation with respect to the etched plate is clearly the same as with respect to a painting: assurance of genuineness can come only from identification of the actual object produced by the artist. But since the several prints from this plate are all genuine instances of the work, however much they differ in color and amount of ink, quality of impression, kind of paper, etc., one might expect here a full parallel between prints and musical performances. Yet there can be prints that are forgeries of the *Tobit Blind* but not performances that are forgeries of the *London Symphony*. The difference is that in the absence of a notation, not only is there no test of correctness of spelling for a plate but there is no test of compliance with a plate for a print. Comparison of a print with a plate, as of two plates, is no more conclusive than is comparison of two pictures. Minute discrepancies may always go unnoticed; and there is no basis for ruling out any of them as inessential. The only way of ascertaining whether a print is genuine is by finding out whether it was taken from a certain plate.[12] A print falsely purporting to have been so produced is in the full sense a forgery of the work.

Here, as earlier, we must be careful not to confuse genuineness with aesthetic merit. That the distinction between original and forgery is aesthetically important does not, we have seen, imply that the original is superior to the forgery. An original painting may be less rewarding than an inspired copy; a damaged original may have lost most of its former merit; an impression from a badly worn plate may be aesthetically much further removed from an early impression than is a good photographic reproduction. Likewise, an incorrect performance, though therefore not strictly an instance of a given quartet at all, may nevertheless—either because the changes improve what the composer wrote or because of sensitive interpretation—be

---

[12] To be original a print must be from a certain plate but need not be printed by the artist. Furthermore, in the case of a woodcut, the artist sometimes only draws upon the block, leaving the cutting to someone else—Holbein's blocks, for example, were usually cut by Lützelberger. Authenticity in an autographic art always depends upon the object's having the requisite, sometimes rather complicated, history of production; but that history does not always include ultimate execution by the original artist.

better than a correct performance.[13] Again, several correct performances of about equal merit may exhibit very different specific aesthetic qualities—power, delicacy, tautness, stodginess, incoherence, etc. Thus even where the constitutive properties of a work are clearly distinguished by means of a notation, they cannot be identified with the aesthetic properties.

Among other arts, sculpture is autographic; cast sculpture is comparable to printmaking while carved sculpture is comparable to painting. Architecture and the drama, on the other hand, are more nearly comparable to music. Any building that conforms to the plans and specifications, any performance of the text of a play in accordance with the stage directions, is as original an instance of the work as any other. But architecture seems to differ from music in that testing for compliance of a building with the specifications requires not that these be pronounced, or transcribed into sound, but that their application be understood. This is true also for the stage directions, as contrasted with the dialogue, of a play. Does this make architecture and the drama less purely allographic arts? Again, an architect's plans seem a good deal like a painter's sketches; and painting is an autographic art. On what grounds can we say that

---

[13] Of course, I am not saying that a correct(ly spelled) performance is correct in any of a number of other usual senses. Nevertheless, the composer or musician is likely to protest indignantly at refusal to accept a performance with a few wrong notes as an instance of a work; and he surely has ordinary usage on his side. But ordinary usage here points the way to disaster for theory (see V,2).

in the one case but not the other a veritable notation is involved? Such questions cannot be answered until we have carried through some rather painstaking analysis.

Since an art seems to be allographic just insofar as it is amenable to notation, the case of the dance is especially interesting. Here we have an art without a traditional notation; and an art where the ways, and even the possibility, of developing an adequate notation are still matters of controversy. Is the search for a notation reasonable in the case of the dance but not in the case of painting? Or, more generally, why is the use of notation appropriate in some arts but not in others? Very briefly and roughly, the answer may be somewhat as follows. Initially, perhaps, all arts are autographic. Where the works are transitory, as in singing and reciting, or require many persons for their production, as in architecture and symphonic music, a notation may be devised in order to transcend the limitations of time and the individual. This involves establishing a distinction between the constitutive and the contingent properties of a work (and in the case of literature, texts have even supplanted oral performances as the primary aesthetic objects). Of course, the notation does not dictate the distinction arbitrarily, but must follow generally—even though it may amend—lines antecedently drawn by the informal classification of performances into works and by practical decisions as to what is prescribed and what is optional. Amenability to notation depends upon a precedent practice that develops only if works of the art in question are commonly either ephemeral or not producible by one person. The dance, like the drama and symphonic and choral music, qualifies on both scores, while painting qualifies on neither.

The general answer to our somewhat slippery second problem of authenticity can be summarized in a few words. A forgery of a work of art is an object falsely purporting to have the history of production requisite for the (or an) original of the work. Where there is a theoretically decisive test for determining that an object has all the constitutive properties of the work in question without determining how or by whom the object was produced, there is no requisite history of production and hence no forgery of any given work. Such a test is provided by a suitable notational system with an articulate set of characters and of relative positions for them. For texts, scores, and perhaps plans, the test is correctness of spelling in this notation; for buildings and performances, the test is compliance with what is correctly spelled. Authority for a notation must be found in an antecedent classification of objects or events into works that cuts across, or admits of a legitimate projection that cuts across, classification by history of production; but definitive identification of works, fully freed from history of production, is achieved only when a notation is established. The allographic art has won its emancipation not by proclamation but by notation.

5. A Task

The two problems of authenticity I have been discussing are rather special and peripheral questions of aesthetics. Answers to them do not amount to an aesthetic theory or even the beginning of one. But failure to answer them can well be the end of one; and their exploration points the way to more basic problems and principles in the general theory of symbols.

Many matters touched upon here need much more careful study. So far, I have only vaguely described, rather than defined, the relations of compliance and of sameness of spelling. I have not examined the features that distinguish notations or notational languages from other languages and from nonlanguages. And I have not discussed the subtle differences between a score, a script, and a sketch. What is wanted now is a fundamental and thoroughgoing inquiry into the nature and function of notation in the arts. This will be undertaken in the next two chapters.

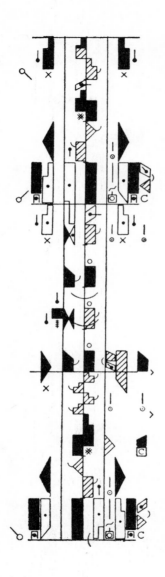

Reverse

Sample of Labanotation. Reproduced with permission of the Dance Notation Bureau, Inc., New York.

IV

THE THEORY OF NOTATION

. . . it is not sufficient to have the whole world at one's disposal—the very infinitude of possibilities cancels out possibilities, as it were, until limitations are discovered.

Roger Sessions*

1. The Primary Function

Concerning notation in the arts there are some questions, often dismissed as mere annoyances, that reach deep into the theory of language and knowledge. Casual speculation on whether a notation for the dance is a legitimate goal, or on why a notation for painting is not, usually stops short of asking what the essential function of a score is, or just what distinguishes a score from a drawing or study or sketch on the one hand and from a verbal description or scenario or script on the other. A score is commonly regarded as a mere tool, no more intrinsic to the finished work than is the sculptor's hammer or the painter's easel. For the score is dispensable after the performance; and music can be composed and learned and played 'by ear', without any score and even by people who cannot read or write any notation. But to take nota-

* "Problems and Issues Facing the Composer Today", in *Problems of Modern Music*, ed. P. H. Lang (New York, W. W. Norton & Co., Inc., 1962), p. 31.

tion as therefore nothing but a practical aid to production is to miss its fundamental theoretical role.

A score, whether or not ever used as a guide for a performance, has as a primary function the authoritative identification of a work from performance to performance. Often scores and notations—and pseudo-scores and pseudo-notations—have such other more exciting functions as facilitating transposition, comprehension, or even composition; but every score, as a score, has the logically prior office of identifying a work.[1] From this derive all the requisite theoretic properties of scores and of the notational systems in which they are written. The first step, then, is to look more closely at this primary function.

First, a score must define a work, marking off the performances that belong to the work from those that do not. This is not to say that the score must provide an easy test for deciding whether a given performance belongs to the work or not; after all, the definition of gold as the element with an atomic weight of 197.2 gives me no ready test for telling a gold piece from a brass one. The line drawn need only be theoretically manifest. What is required is that all and only performances that comply with the score be performances of the work.

But that is not all. Most of the definitions we encounter

---

[1] This is by no means true of everything commonly called a score; here, as with most familiar words, systematic use involves a specialization from ordinary use. The reasons for the choice made in this case will already be apparent from the preceding chapter. Obviously what is commonly called but does not by the above criterion qualify as a score is not thereby disparaged but only reclassified (see further V,2).

IV,1

in ordinary discourse and in formal systems fail to satisfy a more stringent demand imposed by the primary duty of a score. While a good definition always unequivocally determines what objects conform to it, a definition is seldom in turn uniquely determined by each of its instances. If I point to an object and ask you what kind of object it is, you may give any of a wide variety of answers, picking out any class to which the object belongs. Accordingly, in passing alternately (and correctly) from an object to a definition—or predicate or other label—the object complies with (e.g., to "table" or some coextensive term), to another object (e.g., a steel table), to another label (e.g., "steel thing") applying to the second object, and to a third object (e.g., an automobile) complying with the second label, we may pass from one object to another such that no label in the series applies to both; and two labels in the series may differ totally in extension, no one object complying with both.

No such latitude can be tolerated in the case of scores. Scores and performances must be so related that in every chain where each step is either from score to compliant performance or from performance to covering score or from one copy of a score to another correct copy of it, all performances belong to the same work and all copies of scores define the same class of performances. Otherwise, the requisite identification of a work from performance to performance would not be guaranteed; we might pass from a performance to another that is not of the same work, or from a score to another that determines a different—even an entirely disjoint—class of performances. Not only must a score uniquely determine the class of performances belonging to the work, but the score (as a class of copies or inscriptions that so define the work) must be uniquely determined, given a performance and the notational system.

This double demand is indeed a strong one. Its motivation and consequences, and the results of weakening it in various ways, need to be carefully considered. We may begin by asking what the properties are that scores, and the notational systems in which scores are written, must have in order to meet this basic requirement. Study of that question will call for some inquiry into the nature of languages and into the differences between languages and nonlinguistic symbol systems, as well as into the features that distinguish notational systems from other languages, and will mean going into some rather bothersome technical details, but may occasionally expose new aspects of some familiar problems.[2]

2. Syntactic Requirements

The symbol scheme of every notational system is notational, but not every symbol system with a notational scheme is a notational system. What distinguishes the notational systems from the others are certain features of the relationship obtaining between notational scheme and application. "Notation" is commonly used indifferently as

[2] The reader with no background in logic, mathematics, or technical philosophy may well skim or skip the rest of this chapter and rely on gathering from the applications and illustrations in later chapters the principles expounded here.

short for either "notational scheme" or "notational system", and for brevity I shall often take advantage of this convenient vacillation where the context precludes confusion.

What, first, constitutes a notational scheme? Any symbol scheme consists of characters, usually with modes of combining them to form others. Characters are certain classes of utterances or inscriptions or marks. (I shall use "inscription" to include utterances, and "mark" to include inscriptions; an inscription is any mark—visual, auditory, etc.—that belongs to a character.) Now the essential feature of a character in a notation is that its members may be freely exchanged for one another without any syntactical effect; or more literally, since actual marks are seldom moved about and exchanged, that all inscriptions of a given character be syntactically equivalent. In other words, being instances of one character in a notation must constitute a sufficient condition for marks being 'true copies' or replicas [3] of each other, or being spelled the

---

[3] The distinction between a word 'type' and its 'tokens' was stressed by Peirce; see *Collected Papers of Charles Sanders Peirce,* vol. IV, ed. C. Hartshorne and P. Weiss (Cambridge, Mass., Harvard University Press, 1933), p. 423. The type is the universal or class of which marks are instances or members. Although I speak in the present text of a character as a class of marks, this is for me informal parlance admissible only because it can readily be translated into more acceptable language. I prefer (see *SA,* pp. 354–364) to dismiss the type altogether and treat the so-called tokens of a type as *replicas* of one another. An inscription need not be an exact duplicate of another to be a replica, or true copy, of it; indeed, there is in general no degree of similarity that is necessary or sufficient for replicahood. See further the examples discussed later in this section.

same way. And a true copy of a true copy of . . . a true copy of an inscription x must always be a true copy of x. For if the relation of being a true copy is not thus transitive, the basic purpose of a notation is defeated. Requisite separation among characters—and hence among scores—will be lost unless identity is preserved in any chain of true copies.

A necessary condition for a notation, then, is *character-indifference* among the instances of each character. Two marks are character-indifferent if each is an inscription (i.e., belongs to some character) and neither one belongs to any character the other does not. Character-indifference is a typical equivalence-relation: reflexive, symmetric, and transitive. A character in a notation is a most-comprehensive class of character-indifferent inscriptions; that is, a class of marks such that every two are character-indifferent and such that no mark outside the class is character-indifferent with every member of it. In short, a character in a notation is an abstraction class [4] of character-

---

[4] In the terminology of Rudolf Carnap (*Der Logische Aufbau der Welt* [Berlin, Weltkreis-Verlag, 1928], p. 102; English translation by R. A. George entitled *The Logical Structure of the World and Pseudoproblems in Philosophy* [Berkeley, University of California Press, 1967], p. 119) a *similarity-circle* of a relation R is a class such that (1) every two members form an R-pair, and (2) no nonmember forms an R-pair with every member. Where R, as above, is an equivalence-relation, a similarity-circle of R is called an *abstraction-class* of R. No nonmember of an abstraction-class forms an R-pair with any member; for since an equivalence-relation is transitive, a nonmember forming an R-pair with one member would form an R-pair with each member, in violation of condition (2).

indifference among inscriptions. As a result, no mark may belong to more than one character.

That the characters must thus be *disjoint* may not seem very important or striking; but it is an absolutely essential and, I think, rather remarkable feature of notations. It is essential for reasons already explained. Suppose, for example, that a certain mark (Figure 3) belongs to both the

ɑ

Figure 3

first and the fourth letters of the alphabet. Then either every "*a*" and every "*d*" will be syntactically equivalent with this mark and hence with each other, so that the two letter-classes collapse into one character, or else joint membership in a letter-class will not guarantee syntactical equivalence, so that instances of the same letter may not be true copies of one another. In neither case will the letters qualify as characters in a notation.

The disjointness of the characters is also somewhat surprising since we have in the world not a realm of inscriptions neatly sorted into clearly separate classes but, rather, a bewildering miscellany of marks differing from each other in all ways and degrees. To impose a partitioning into disjoint sets seems a willful even though needful violence. And no matter how characters are specified, there will almost inevitably be many marks for which it will be difficult or even virtually impossible to decide whether or not they belong to a given character. The more delicate and precise the stipulated differentiation between characters (e.g., suppose characters are classes of straight marks differing in length by one-millionth of an inch), the harder will it be to determine whether certain marks belong to one character or another. If, on the other hand, there are wide neutral zones between characters (e.g., suppose that the characters are: the class of straight marks between one and two inches long, the class of straight marks between five and six inches long, etc.), then among the marks that do not belong to any character will be some that are exceedingly difficult to distinguish from some instances of some character. There is no way of preventing this infiltration at the borders, no way of ensuring that due caution will protect against all mistakes in identifying a mark as belonging or not belonging to a given character. But this trouble is not peculiar to notations; it is a pervasive and inescapable fact of experience. And it by no means precludes establishment of a system of disjoint classes of marks; it only makes hard the determination of the membership of some marks in such classes.

Obviously anyone designing a notation will try to minimize the probability of errors. But this is a technological concern, differing sharply from the theoretical requirement of disjointness. What distinguishes a genuine notation is not how easily correct judgments can be made but what their consequences are. The crucial point here is that for a genuine notation, as contrasted with a nondisjoint classification, marks correctly judged to be joint members of a character will always be true copies of one another.

The distinction stands even where correct judgments under a given nondisjoint scheme are relatively easy to make, while those under a given genuine notation are so inordinately difficult as to make it useless.

Yet the difficulty can no longer be dismissed as merely technological when it goes beyond insurmountability in practice and becomes impossibility in principle. So long as the differentiation between characters is finite, no matter how minute, the determination of membership of mark in character will depend upon the acuteness of our perceptions and the sensitivity of the instruments we can devise. But if the differentiation is not finite, if there are two characters such that for some mark no even theoretically workable test could determine that the mark does not belong to both characters, then keeping the characters separate is not just practically but theoretically impossible. Suppose, for example, that only straight marks are concerned, and that marks differing in length by even the smallest fraction of an inch are stipulated to belong to different characters. Then no matter how precisely the length of any mark is measured, there will always be two (indeed, infinitely many) characters, corresponding to different rational numbers, such that the measurement will fail to determine that the mark does not belong to them. For a notational scheme, not only must sameness of spelling be preserved where error is avoided but error must be at least theoretically avoidable.

The second requirement upon a notational scheme, then, is that the characters be *finitely differentiated*, or *articulate*. It runs: *For every two characters K and K' and every* mark *m that does not actually belong to both, determination either that m does not belong to K or that m does not belong to K' is theoretically possible.* "Theoretically possible" may be interpreted in any reasonable way; whatever the choice, all logically and mathematically grounded impossibility (as in examples given below) will of course be excluded.

Finite differentiation neither implies nor is implied by a finite number of characters. On the one hand, a scheme may provide for an infinite number of finitely differentiated characters, as in Arabic fractional notation.[5] On the other hand, a scheme may consist of just two characters that are not finitely differentiated—for example, suppose all marks not longer than one inch belong to one character, and all longer marks belong to the other.

A scheme is syntactically dense if it provides for infinitely many characters so ordered that between each two there is a third. In such a scheme, our second requirement is violated everywhere: no mark can be determined to belong to one rather than to many other characters. But as we have just seen, absence of density does not guarantee finite differentiation; even a completely discontinuous [6]

[5] I am speaking here of symbols only, not of numbers or anything else the symbols may stand for. The Arabic fractional numerals are finitely differentiated even though fractional quantities are not. See further section 5 below.

[6] The distinction between density or compactness and continuity— between the rational and the real numbers—need not trouble us much here; for a dense scheme, whether continuous or not, is undifferentiated in the extreme. Since I reserve "discrete" for non-overlapping between individuals, I shall call a scheme that contains

scheme may be undifferentiated throughout. And of course a completely or partially discontinuous scheme may be locally undifferentiated; our second requirement is violated wherever there is even a single mark that does not belong to two characters and yet is such that determination of its nonmembership in at least one of them is theoretically impossible.

The syntactic requirements of disjointness and of finite differentiation are clearly independent of each other. The first but not the second is satisfied by the scheme of classification of straight marks that counts every difference in length, however small, as a difference of character. The second but not the first is satisfied by a scheme where all inscriptions are conspicuously different but some two characters have at least one inscription in common.

None of this should be taken as suggesting that character-indifference—or syntactical equivalence, or being a true copy or a replica of—between marks is any simple function of shape, size, etc. The letter-classes of our alphabet, for example, are established by tradition and habit; and defining them would be as hard as defining such ordinary terms as "desk" and "table". Plainly, having the same shape, size, etc., is neither necessary nor sufficient for two marks to belong to the same letter. A given "a" (Figure 4, left) may be much less like another (Figure 4, cen-

---

no dense subscheme "completely discontinuous" or "discontinuous throughout". "Dense" and "discontinuous" are of course short for "densely ordered" and "discontinuously ordered"; a given set may be dense under one ordering and discontinuous throughout under another (see further note 17 below).

ɑ A d

Figure 4

ter) than like a given "d" (Figure 4, right) or "o". Furthermore, two marks of identical shape and size may, as a result of context, belong to different characters (Figure 5).

ɑɑ
ɑd

Figure 5

Indeed, it may even happen that the one of two marks that looks in isolation more like an "a" may count as a "d" while the one that looks more like a "d" counts as an "a" (Figure 6).

bɑɑ
mɑn

Figure 6

These cases cause no real trouble; for neither of our conditions demands any specific difference between inscriptions of different characters, or prohibits use of context in determining membership of a mark in a character.

But what of a mark that, equivocally, reads as different letters when placed in different contexts at different times? Disjointness is violated if any mark belongs to two different characters, whether at the same time or at different times. Thus if the alphabet is to qualify as a notation, not such enduring marks but, rather, unequivocal time-slices of them must be taken as members of the characters—that is, as inscriptions of letters.[7]

When a symbolic scheme is given in use rather than by specific definition, satisfaction of the requirements for a

---

[7] In other cases, two simultaneous contexts endow a mark with different readings: for example, in billboard language, the center mark in

$$\begin{matrix} & b & \\ a & d & d \\ & d & \end{matrix}$$

reads down as an instance of one letter and across as an instance of another. Now this equivocal mark is not character-indifferent either with all "a"s or with all "d"s (for not all exhibit this duplicity); and the mark cannot be counted as both an "a" and a "d" without sacrificing syntactic equivalence among the instances of each of these letters and violating the condition of disjointness. Nor are time-slices of the mark any less equivocal. Rather, this mark, if an inscription at all, is an instance not of any usual letter of the alphabet but of an additional character. Again, consider cases of shifting and of multiple orientation. Where sanctioned changes in orientation make a mark sometimes a "d" and sometimes a "b", unequivocal time-slices rather than the enduring mark qualify as inscriptions in the notation. Where a mark is simultaneously multiply oriented—legitimately subject to different readings from different directions at once—it may belong to a character consisting of all marks having the same multiple orientation and readings.

notation has to be judged by observation of practice. If there are alternative, equally good formulations of that practice, the conditions may be satisfied under some but not others among these formulations. But how is the second condition to be interpreted in application to a traditional scheme like the alphabet? That we have no explicit procedure for determining whether a given mark does or does not belong to any given letter hardly means that finite differentiation is lacking. Rather, we adopt a policy of admitting no mark as an inscription of a letter unless or until we can decide that the mark belongs to no other letter. In effect, we impose finite differentiation by excluding the undecidable cases; and the policy must be incorporated in any appropriate specification of the scheme. This does not hold for all schemes; with a dense scheme, the result would be to eliminate all inscriptions. But where membership of only some rather than all marks in each character is undecidable, the policy is normal and is to be assumed for all schemes not given by or plainly calling for a specification that precludes it.

The syntactic requirements of disjointness and finite differentiation are met by our familiar alphabetical, numerical, binary, telegraphic, and basic musical notations; and by a wide variety of other describable notations, some of them having purely academic interest. On the other hand, we shall see that some schemes recently devised and called notations fail, because they do not meet these minimum demands, to qualify as notations at all. The two requirements are not meant to describe the class of what are ordinarily called notations, but are rather conditions that must be fulfilled if the basic theoretic purpose of a score is to be served. They will accordingly enable us to draw certain critical distinctions among types of symbol scheme; but I shall come back to this later.

3. Composition of Characters

In most symbol schemes, inscriptions may be combined in certain ways to make other inscriptions. An inscription is *atomic* if it contains no other inscription; otherwise it is *compound*. When a scheme is not newly prescribed but is already before us for description, we have some latitude in what we take as atoms and how we frame the rule of combination. Sometimes the happiest analysis readily makes itself evident; in the usual alphabetical notation, for example, letter-inscriptions (including blanks or spaces separating strings of letters) are best taken as atomic; and sequences of these—ranging from two-letter inscriptions up through entire discourses—as compound. On the other hand, for ordinary musical notation the analysis into atomic inscriptions and modes of combination is more complex and less immediately indicated. The most useful treatment here calls for atoms sorted into categories (note-signs, clef-signs, time-signs, etc.) and for rules that not only make reference to these categories but provide for combination in two dimensions. An intermediate case might be a scheme where the only mode of combination is linear concatenation of atomic inscriptions of a category but where certain sequences are excluded—say on grounds of length or of particular unwanted juxtaposition—as inscriptions in the scheme. In English, for example, not all strings of letters are words. But such exclusion of certain combinations must not be confused with admitting them but giving them no application—a semantic matter I shall come to presently.

In virtually no feasible scheme is every sum of inscriptions an inscription. The component inscriptions must stand to each other in the relationship prescribed by the governing rules of combination. Thus even where unrestricted concatenation is authorized, a sum of scattered inscriptions does not in general constitute an inscription.

A *character* is atomic or compound according as its instances are atomic or compound. The requirements for a notation apply to compound as well as to atomic characters. The character "jup" and the character "j" must be disjoint even though one contains the other. The paradox here is superficial. No inscription of any character may be an inscription of the other (and, indeed, no "jup" is a "j", and no "j" is a "jup"); but inscriptions of one character may be parts of or otherwise overlap inscriptions of another (as every "jup" has a "j" as part). Even inscriptions of different *atomic* characters may have common parts so long as no such part is an inscription in the scheme; that is, atomic inscriptions need be discrete relative to the notation in question only, as the "a" and the "e" in Figure 7 are

Figure 7

atomic and discrete in a scheme that recognizes no proper part of either as an inscription.[8]

To say that a character is composed of certain others is to be understood as short for saying that each member of the character is composed of inscriptions of certain other characters. Occasionally, however, full and explicit statement pays its way. The character "add" is awkwardly described as consisting of the character "a" followed by the character "d" 'taken twice'—or by the character "d" followed by itself. It is better described as the class of inscriptions each of which consists of an "a" (-inscription) followed by a "d" followed by another "d".

4. Compliance

A symbol system consists of a symbol scheme correlated with a field of reference. Although we have seen (II) that a symbol may or may not denote what it refers to, I am concerned in this chapter with denotation rather than exemplification. But "denotation" must be taken somewhat more broadly than is usual, to cover a system where scores are correlated with performances complying with them, or words with their pronunciations, as well as a system

---

[8] Technical treatment of discreteness, overlapping, etc., will be found in *SA*, pp. 46–61, 117–118. Note how far astray is the usual idea that the elements of a notation must be discrete. First, *characters* of a notation, as classes, must rather be disjoint; discreteness is a relation among individuals. Second, *inscriptions* of a notation need not be discrete at all. And finally, even atomic inscriptions of different characters need be discrete relative to that notation only.

where words are correlated with what they apply to or name. Partly as a way of keeping this in mind, I shall use "complies with" as interchangeable with "is denoted by", "has as a compliant" as interchangeable with "denotes", and "compliance-class" as interchangeable with "extension".[9] Compliance requires no special conformity; whatever is denoted by a symbol complies with it.

Basically, compliance is with an inscription. In a given system, many things may comply with a single inscription, and the class of these constitutes the compliance-class of the inscription under that system. Of course, the compliance-class normally does not itself comply with the inscription; its members do. An inscription having classes as compliants has a class of classes as its compliance-class.

Convenient illustrations of some technical terms and distinctions may be cited from what I shall for short call *sound-English*, where ordinary English alphabetical notation is correlated with sound-events according to the usual practice of pronunciation, and what I shall call *object-English*, where the correlation is rather with objects (including events, etc.) according to the usual practice of application. The illustrations will depend, of course, upon some tacit but obvious arbitrary decisions concerning, and occasionally upon some simplification of, usual practice.[10]

---

[9] This is *not* to say that the extension of a word includes *both* its pronunciations and the objects it applies to; for the extension of a symbol is always relative to a system, and in no normal or useful system is a word correlated with both its pronunciations and its applicata.

[10] Formulation of rules of correlation, like resolution of inscriptions into atoms, is seldom uniquely determined for a given natural lan-

COMPLIANCE

Some inscriptions, even some atomic ones, may have no compliants; in object-English, neither a "ktn" nor a "k" has any compliant. Not only may compound inscriptions happen to be the least units with any compliants but an inscription compounded of inscriptions that have compliants may or may not have compliants; in object-English, though "green" and "horse" have compliants, "green horse" does not. Inscriptions without compliants may be called *vacant*. Vacancy may arise either from a character having been assigned no compliant, or from there being no such compliants as are called for, or from explicit stipulation that the character have no compliant. A vacant inscription belongs as truly to the symbol scheme as does any other, and may be as big and black; its lack is semantic, not syntactic. An object complying with no inscription is unlabeled in the system.

Correlation of a scheme with a field of reference normally involves not merely particular correlation of inscriptions with objects but also correlation of modes of inscription-combination with relationships among objects. For example, left-right succession of letter-inscriptions in sound-English is correlated with temporal succession of sounds. Even where both a compound inscription and components of it have compliants, compliants of the compound may or may not be composed suitably (or at all) of compliants of the components; in sound-English, for example, a compliant of a "ch" is not a sequence of a com-

---

guage, but depends on how the language is analyzed and described. When we speak of 'a language' we are often speaking elliptically of a language under some such systematic formulation.

pliant of a "c" and a compliant of an "h". Where each
compliant of a compound inscription is a whole made up
of compliants of component inscriptions, and these compliants of components stand in the relation called for by
the correlation in question between modes of inscription-
combination and certain relationships among objects, the
whole inscription is *composite*. Any other nonvacant inscription is *prime*.

All composite inscriptions are compound, but not all
(even nonvacant) compound inscriptions are composite.
Inversely, all nonvacant atomic inscriptions are prime, but
not all prime inscriptions are atomic. "Composite" is the
semantic counterpart of the syntactic term "compound",
but the semantic term "prime" is only partially parallel to
the syntactic term "atomic"; for while no proper part of

SYNTACTIC CLASSIFICATION

| | | Inscriptions | | Other Marks |
		Atomic	Compound	
SEMANTIC CLASSIFICATION	Vacant	e.g. a "k" in object-English	e.g. a "ktn" (also a "square circle") in object-Eng- lish	Includes ill-formed sequences, fragments of inscriptions, and all other marks not belonging to any character
	Prime	e.g. an "o" in sound-English	e.g. a "ch" in sound-English	
	Composite	////////	e.g. a "bo" in sound-English	

Figure 8

an atomic inscription is an inscription, parts of a prime inscription may have compliants. The inscription is prime in that compliants of its parts, combined in the specified way, do not make up a compliant of the whole.

This profusion of terminology and technicalities will perhaps be rendered a little more tractable by the tabulation in Figure 8.

A mark that is unequivocally an inscription of a single character is nevertheless *ambiguous* if it has different compliants at different times or in different contexts, whether its several ranges result from different literal or from literal and metaphorical uses. More strictly of course we should say, where the variance is with time, that different time-slices of the mark have different compliance-classes; and where the variance is with simultaneous contexts, that the mark is semantically related in different ways to two or more inscriptions containing it.[11]

A character is ambiguous if any inscription of it is; but even if every inscription of a character is unambiguous, the character is ambiguous unless all its inscriptions have the same compliance-class. An unambiguous character is vacant, prime, or composite according as its inscriptions are; and the common compliance-class of its inscriptions may be considered the compliance-class of the character. Indeed, since the inscriptions of an unambiguous character are thus semantically as well as syntactically equivalent, we can usually speak of the character and its compliance-

---

[11] Compare the treatment of equivocal marks in section 2 above. Unambiguity can be achieved by dividing up inscriptions, or characters, in certain ways; but then syntactic equivalence will be made to depend upon semantic considerations.

class without bothering to distinguish among its several instances.

But since two inscriptions of an ambiguous character may have different compliance-classes, syntactic equivalence implies semantic equivalence in unambiguous systems only. In neither ambiguous nor unambiguous systems does semantic equivalence imply syntactic equivalence. Inscriptions having the same compliance-class may belong to different characters; and different unambiguous characters may have the same compliance-class. Syntactical distinctness is not dissolved by semantic equivalence.

5. Semantic Requirements

The first semantic requirement upon notational systems is that they be *unambiguous*; for obviously the basic purpose of a notational system can be served only if the compliance relationship is invariant.[12] Any ambiguous *inscription* must be excluded since it will give conflicting decisions concerning whether some object complies with it. Any ambiguous *character* must be excluded, even if its

---

[12] Whether a system is ambiguous will depend not only upon just what marks are taken as its inscriptions and just how these are classified into characters, as we have seen above, but also upon just what correlation between marks and objects is taken as constituting compliance. In sound-English, for example, "c" is naturally regarded as ambiguous since some "c"s are soft and others hard. But we could take "c" as unambiguous, with the soft c-sounds as the compliants of all "c"s—even those in "ct"s. Characters such as "ct" would then be prime. The choice here is between different descriptions of the language. In what follows, I shall often tacitly assume that such decisions have been made in a way that is apparent from the context.

inscriptions are all unambiguous; for since different inscriptions of it will have different compliants, some inscriptions that count as true copies of each other will have different compliance-classes. In either case, identity of work will not be preserved in every chain of steps from performance to covering score and from score to compliant performance.

Two further semantic requirements upon notational systems parallel but do not follow from the syntactic requirements.

Even though all characters of a symbol system be disjoint classes of unambiguous inscriptions, and all inscriptions of any one character have the same compliance-class,

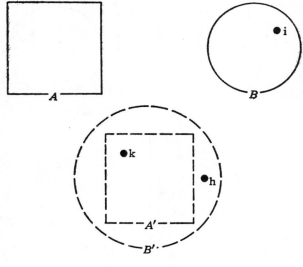

Figure 9

different compliance-classes may intersect in any way. *But in a notational system, the compliance-classes must be disjoint.* For if two different compliance-classes intersect, some inscription will have two compliants such that one belongs to a compliance-class that the other does not; and a chain from compliant to inscription to compliant will thus lead from a member of one compliance-class to something outside that class. For example, in Figure 9, if *A* and *B* stand for characters, and *A'* and *B'* for their compliance-classes, with *A'* included in *B'*, then *k* in *A'* is also in *B'* and complies with inscription *i*, which in turn has as a compliant *h*, which is not in *A'*. Where neither of two intersecting compliance-classes is included in the other, a chain

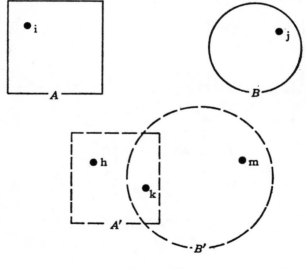

Figure 10

from compliant to inscription to compliant to inscription to compliant may connect two objects that do not even belong to any one compliance-class. For example, in Figure 10, h complies with i, which in turn has k as a compliant; k complies also with j, which has m as another compliant. But h and m belong to no one compliance-class. Thus any intersection of different compliance-classes defeats the primary purpose of a notational system.

Must different characters, furthermore, have different compliance-classes? That is, must a system be free of redundancy? In a redundant system, some inscription will have a compliant that also complies with a second inscription that is not a true copy of the first.[13] Accordingly, while in every chain of permitted steps every compliant will belong to the same compliance-class, not in every such chain will every inscription belong to the same character. Hence, strictly, redundancy must be proscribed. Yet insofar as preserving identity of character (e.g., of score from copy to copy) is incidental to preserving identity of compliance-class (e.g., of musical work from performance to performance), redundancy is harmless. And of course redundancy in a system is easily removed by discarding all but one of any set of coextensive terms. In any case, nonredundancy need not be taken as a separate requirement. We may consider the *disjointness requirement* to stipulate *that no two characters have any compliant in common*; so

---

[13] Redundancy is the dual of ambiguity. Ambiguity consists of multiplicity of compliance-classes for one character; redundancy consists of multiplicity of characters for one compliance-class. But, of course, with no ambiguity a character may apply to many objects; and with no redundancy an object may comply with many inscriptions.

IV,5

that not only must every two different compliance-classes in a notational system be disjoint but every two characters must have different compliance-classes. Nevertheless, for two characters to have all as against only some common compliants is often the lesser transgression.

Although each two characters in a purely notational system must be semantically quite separate, compliants of one character may be parts of or properly overlap compliants of another. Semantic disjointness of characters no more implies discreteness of compliants than syntactic disjointness of characters implies discreteness of inscriptions. "State in the U.S." and "county in the U.S.", as applying to certain geographical regions, are semantically disjoint even though every compliant of the one contains several compliants of the other.

The requirement of semantic disjointness rules out most ordinary languages, even if we suppose them freed of ambiguity. For see how much is prohibited. A notational system cannot contain any pair of semantically intersecting terms like "doctor" and "Englishman"; and if the system contains the term "man", for example, it cannot contain the more specific term "Englishman" or the more general term "animal". The characters of a notational system are semantically segregated.

The final requirement for a notational system is *semantic finite differentiation; that is, for every two characters K and K' such that their compliance-classes are not identical, and every object h that does not comply with both, determination either that h does not comply with K or that h does not comply with K' must be theoretically possible.*

This condition again appreciably narrows the class of systems that qualify as notational. Consider, for example, a system consisting of fully reduced Arabic fractional numerals taking as compliants physical objects according to their weights in fractions of an ounce. The syntactic requirements of disjointness and finite differentiation, and the semantic requirements of unambiguity and disjointness, are met here; but since no limit is set upon significant difference in weight, there will always be many characters such that not even the finest measurement can attest that an object does not comply with them all. Thus the system is not notational.

The particular system just described is semantically dense (that is, provides for an infinite number of characters with compliance-classes so ordered that between each two there is a third), and everywhere violates the fifth condition. But the condition may also be violated everywhere in some systems that are semantically discontinuous throughout—i.e., nowhere semantically dense. In other systems that are semantically discontinuous throughout or in part, violation may be local rather than pervasive. A system for which each reduced Arabic fraction takes as compliants all and only those objects of the indicated weight that are identical with the Cullinan diamond (so that the field of reference consists of but a single object) is still not semantically differentiated.[14] And if a system contains two characters "*a*" and "*b*", and all objects weigh-

---

[14] Hereafter, I shall often write "differentiated" as short for "finitely differentiated". The convenient alternative term "articulate" will be more often used later in the book.

ing an ounce or less comply with "*a*" while all objects weighing more comply with "*b*", then that system—no matter what other characters and reference-classes it may embrace—lacks semantic differentiation and fails of notationality.

6. Notations

The five stated requirements for a notational system are all negative and general, satisfiable by systems with null or even no characters. These requirements are designed to preclude otherwise inevitable trouble, not to ensure a vocabulary or grammar adequate for a given subject-matter. They are somewhat like a building code that legislates against faults in construction without prescribing the accommodations needed for particular families.

A good many other features that might be thought essential are not covered either. No requirement of a manageably small or even finite set of atomic characters, no requirement of clarity, of legibility, of durability, of maneuverability, of ease of writing or reading, of graphic suggestiveness, of mnemonic efficacy, or of ready duplicability or performability has been imposed. These may be highly desirable properties, and to some degree even necessary for any practicable notation; and the study of such engineering matters could be fascinating and profitable. But none of this has anything to do with the basic theoretical function of notational systems.

Throughout, I have been stressing the nominative or predicative aspect of symbols, not their assertive or imperative or interrogative force, and have taken characters more as predicates or labels than as sentences. This is natural in the present context; for in notational systems the grammatical mood of a character seldom matters much. In sound-English, for example, a string of letters may stand for a certain sequence of sounds; but to add that the string declares that such sounds occur in such sequence, or commands that they should, would be quite gratuitous. No one asks whether the string of letters is true or false, and no one says to it "Yes, sir!" or "No, I won't." Offhand, one might guess that absence of grammatical mood is a distinguishing feature of notational systems; but actually it is not. Suppose, for instance, that operators were added to a notational system so that, say, while "vo" stands for a *v*-sound followed by an *o*-sound, "†vo" asserts that a *v*-sound is followed by an *o*-sound, "!vo" commands that a *v*-sound be followed by an *o*-sound, and "?vo" asks whether a *v*-sound is followed by an *o*-sound. The system does not thereby cease to be notational. Conversely, object-English deprived of sentences and restricted to phrases does not thereby become notational. The point is that just as tense is irrelevant to languages insofar as they are logical, so mood is irrelevant insofar as they are notational. Mere absence or presence of tense does not make a system logical or unlogical; and mere absence or presence of mood does not make a system notational or non-notational.

I have been further simplifying by speaking usually as if the only predicates involved were one-place predicates of individuals. To cover cases where either many-place predicates or predicates of classes need to be taken into account, without altering the statement of any of our five requirements, about all we need do is to include sequences and classes along with individuals among the 'objects' that may be compliants of characters.[15]

In sum, the properties required of a notational system are unambiguity and syntactic and semantic disjointness and differentiation. These are in no sense merely recommended for a good and useful notation but are features that distinguish notational systems—good or bad—from non-notational systems. All derive from the primary purpose a score must serve; and all are categorically required for any even theoretically workable notational system. A system is notational, then, if and only if all objects complying with inscriptions of a given character belong to the same compliance class and we can, theoretically, determine that each mark belongs to, and each object complies with inscriptions of, at most one particular character.

The five conditions are mutually independent in the usual logical sense that satisfaction or violation of one or more of them does not imply satisfaction or violation of any of the others. And although the conditions were designed to define notational systems, other important types of symbol system are distinguished by violation of certain combinations of these conditions.

[15] The way of formulating a nominalistically acceptable version of our five requirements is rather obvious so long as all the predicates involved, whether one-place or many-place, are predicates of individuals; and the nominalist need not allow for ineliminable predicates of classes since he will not construe any admissible language as containing such predicates.

The intricate, abstract, and probably trying technical study pursued in the foregoing pages of this chapter has thus provided means for analyzing and for comparing and contrasting in significant ways the varied systems of symbolization used in art, science, and life in general. Before returning to specific questions pertaining to symbolism in the arts, I want to look at some systems from other fields.

7. Clocks and Counters

Suppose we have a simple pressure gauge with a circular face and a single pointer that moves smoothly clockwise as the pressure increases. If there are no figures or other marks on the face, and every difference in pointer position constitutes a difference in character, the instrument is not using a notation in reporting pressure to us. The requirement of syntactic differentiation is not met; for we can never determine the position of the pointer with absolute precision. And since the semantic ordering—of pressures—is also dense, semantic as well as syntactic differentiation is lacking.

If the dial is graduated by dots into, say, fifty divisions, is the symbol scheme now used notational? That depends upon how the gauge is to be read. If absolute position of the pointer on the face is what counts, the dots being used only as aids in approximate determination of that position, the scheme remains undifferentiated both syntactically and semantically. A notational scheme is indeed present, but the characters (the graduation-dots) of this notation are not the characters (the absolute pointer positions) of the symbol scheme of the gauge. Rather, the dots belong to an auxiliary scheme useful for locating approximately where the pointer is.

On the other hand, suppose the same dial is to be read differently, with each dot taken as marking the center of a region such that any appearance of the pointer within that region counts as an inscription of the same character. This scheme will be notational provided the fifty regions taken are disjoint and separated by some gaps, however small. And the system will be notational provided the ranges of pressure correlated with the fifty characters are also disjoint and separated by gaps, however small.

These are not artificial alternatives. Concrete examples are before us many times a day. Consider an ordinary watch without a second-hand. The hour-hand is normally used only to pick out one of twelve divisions of the half-day. It speaks notationally. So does the minute-hand if used only to pick out one of sixty divisions of the hour; but if the absolute distance of the minute-hand beyond the preceding mark is taken as indicating the absolute time elapsed since that mark was passed, the symbol system is non-notational. Of course, if we set some limit—whether of a half-minute or one second or less—upon the fineness of judgment so to be made, the scheme here too may become notational. On a watch with a second-hand, the minute-hand is read notationally, and the second-hand may be read either way.

But now suppose the field of reference is of a quite different sort, and our instruments report not on pressure or time but upon the number of dimes dropped into a toy bank having a total capacity of fifty dimes. If the count is reported by an Arabic numeral displayed in an aperture, the system is clearly notational. But what if the indicator is rather a pointer as in our pressure gauges? If every position on the circumference is taken as a character, whether or not the dial is graduated, the system—as in the case of the first pressure gauges described above—will be semantically as well as syntactically undifferentiated. Full distinguishability of elements in the field of reference does not of itself guarantee semantic differentiation; indeed, if there is only one object and if determining which of two characters it complies with is theoretically impossible, semantic differentiation is lacking. Incidentally, the counter so read will also be highly inefficient; for we can never tell from it just how many dimes have been deposited, and if each number of dimes is correlated with only one character, infinitely many atomic characters will be vacant. If we take the many positions within a given region as different characters correlated with the same number of dimes, then the system is redundant and so lacks semantic disjointness as well. However, if the counter with a graduated face is so read that there are just fifty syntactically disjoint and differentiated characters, and each is correlated with a different number of dimes, the system will be notational.

8. Analogs and Digits

The pressure gauge first described above is a pure and elementary example of what is called an analog computer. The dime-counter displaying numerals is a simple example of what is called a digital computer; and an ordinary watch, read in the most usual way, combines analog and digital computers. But the difference between analog and digital machines or systems is easier to illustrate than to define, and some current notions about it are mistaken. Plainly, a digital system has nothing special to do with digits, or an analog system with analogy. The characters of a digital system may have objects or events of any kind as their inscriptions; and the compliants under an analog system may be as remote and different as we please from the characters. If one-one correlation between characters and compliance-classes makes a system analog, then digital systems also qualify as analog. Since the misleading traditional terms "analog" and "digital" are unlikely to be discarded, perhaps the best course is to try to dissociate them from analogy and digits and a good deal of loose talk, and distinguish them in terms of density and differentiation—though these are not opposites.

A symbol *scheme* is analog if syntactically dense; a *system* is analog if syntactically and semantically dense. Analog systems are thus both syntactically and semantically undifferentiated in the extreme: for every character there are infinitely many others such that for some mark, we cannot possibly determine that the mark does not belong to all, and such that for some object we cannot possibly determine that the object does not comply with all. A system of this kind is obviously the very antithesis of a notational system. But density, while it implies, is not implied by complete lack of differentiation; and a system is analog only if dense.

ANALOGS AND DIGITS

A digital scheme, in contrast, is discontinuous throughout; and in a digital system the characters of such a scheme are one-one correlated with compliance-classes of a similarly discontinuous set. But discontinuity, though implied by, does not imply differentiation; for as we have seen, a system with only two characters may be syntactically and semantically undifferentiated throughout. To be digital a system must be not merely discontinuous but *differentiated* throughout, syntactically and semantically. If, as we assume for systems now under discussion, it is also unambiguous and syntactically and semantically disjoint, it will therefore be notational.

Digital computers are sometimes said to be capable of complete precision while analog computers can achieve at best only a good approximation.[16] This is true only insofar as the task of the digital computer is counting while that of the analog computer is registering absolute position in a continuum. The real virtues of digital instruments are those of notational systems: definiteness and repeatability of readings. Analog instruments may offer greater sensitivity and flexibility. With an analog instrument we are not fettered by an arbitrary lower boundary of discrimination; the only limit upon the fineness of our readings is the (varying) limit upon our accuracy in determining, say, the position of a pointer. However, once the maximum required fineness of discrimination has been settled,

---

[16] See, however, the discussion in John von Neumann, "The General and Logical Theory of Automata", in *Cerebral Mechanisms in Behavior*, ed. Lloyd A. Jeffress (New York, John Wiley & Sons, Inc., 1951), pp. 7ff.

we can construct a digital instrument (if we can construct any instrument) that will give readings that fine. Where the task is gauging or measuring, the analog instrument is likely to play its chief role in the exploratory stages, before units of measurement have been fixed; then a suitably designed digital instrument takes over.

If only thoroughly dense systems are analog, and only thoroughly differentiated ones digital, many systems are of neither type. Some of these are either syntactically or semantically differentiated but not both; and some, although both syntactically and semantically undifferentiated, are yet not both syntactically and semantically dense. When a system is syntactically but not semantically dense, as in the case of our counter with the unmarked dial, the result is commonly but not inevitably (see VI, note 7) either vast waste or vast redundancy: either many vacant characters or huge sets of coextensive characters. When a system is semantically but not syntactically dense, the result may be inadequacy or ambiguity: either some wanted compliance-classes being left nameless or many sharing the same name. In any event, systems of such mongrel types seldom survive long in computer practice; the drive is towards the matching of syntactic with semantic properties that is peculiar to analog and digital systems. If the subject-matter is antecedently atomized, we tend to adopt an articulate symbol scheme and a digital system. Or if we are predisposed to apply an available articulate symbol scheme to a previously undifferentiated field, we try to provide the symbols with differentiated compliance-classes by dividing, combining, deleting; the fractional quantities not registered by our meter tend to be disregarded, and the smallest units it discriminates to be taken as the atomic units of what is measured. Should a prior structuring authoritatively resist such surgery, we may lay aside our articulate symbol scheme and turn to an analog system. Here as elsewhere the development and application of symbol systems is a dynamic process of analysis and organization; and the tensions that arise may be resolved by adjustment on either side of the system until an equilibrium is at least temporarily established.

Apart from computer applications, systems that are neither analog nor digital are common. Consider, for example, the terms "halfway between *a* and *b*", "halfway between *a* and halfway between *a* and *b*", "halfway between *b* and halfway between *a* and *b*", "halfway between *a* and halfway between *a* and halfway between *a* and *b*", and so on without limit. This system is syntactically differentiated but semantically dense [17]; its compliance-

---

[17] The syntactic ordering of these terms (beginning with one-letter terms alphabetically ordered, proceeding to two-letter terms alphabetically ordered, and so on) is discontinuous throughout, and also the system is syntactically differentiated; yet the ordering of these terms according to the semantic property of left-right position of the compliant points is dense, and the system is semantically undifferentiated throughout. A similar example cited earlier was that of Arabic rational numerals taking as compliants physical objects according to weight in fractions of an ounce; the syntactic ordering here derives from the order of the digits, the semantic from the order of increasing weight. Only because density and discontinuity depend upon ordering can a single system of characters, differently ordered, be syntactically discontinuous throughout and semantically dense, or syntactically dense and semantically discontinuous throughout. Systems of the latter sort cannot, of course, be found among languages, which are—whether natural or notational—always syntactically differenti-

classes are the (unit-classes of) points on a line segment. And far from being manufactured to serve as an illustration, the system is part of ordinary English. Everything depends here, of course, upon provision for unlimited compounding of characters out of others. Where, as with a computer, there is a limit to the length of message—e.g., number of decimal places, etc.—that can be produced, no unambiguous system with a notational scheme can have a dense set of compliance-classes.[18]

9. Inductive Translation

Among the many ways a computer may process messages are *deletion* and *supplementation*. The first occurs, for example, where a curve is scanned and the positions of some points on it reported. The second occurs where some points are fed in and a curve or other points on it produced, whether by interpolation or extrapolation. Deletion is often but not always or exclusively involved in translation from analog into digital messages, and supplementation in translation from digital into analog messages. Some important functions of symbols are illustrated in the process of supplementation.

---

ated; but an example from among nonlinguistic systems has been cited above (section 7) in the system of the ungraduated counter with every point on the circumference constituting a character, and more important examples will be encountered below (VI,2).

[18] A given computer is always thus limited; but so also, in view of mortality, is a given speaker. The decimal system in general, or the English language, imposes no such limits.

Consider machines designed to receive two or more points and supply others. A crude machine might simply select [19] each point by spinning a wheel or casting dice. The choices cannot be said to be based in any way upon the data; the available evidence is utterly ignored. At the opposite extreme, a machine might be so constructed as to handle straight lines only. Any two points will then determine a line and thereby all points to be interpolated and extrapolated. Far from being ignored, the data dictate all remaining points by dictating the choice of line. If the first machine was little more than a roulette wheel, the second is a simple calculator like an adding machine.

Now consider a computer capable of handling curves of various types. When the data are compatible with several of these curves, how shall the machine decide? Even if it now resorts to wheel-spinning or dice-throwing, it still differs radically from our first machine; for this one, like the second, chooses among curves rather than points and rejects curves incompatible with the evidence. If a linear order of preference among curves is given and the machine is instructed to choose the remaining curve highest on that scale, chance will not enter at all. Or such a scale may be used merely to weight the odds so that the choice, though made by wheel or dice, will not be purely random. Yet in all these cases, the machine operates independently

---

[19] "Selects", "chooses", "decides", etc., in the present context do not imply any deliberation but mean only "gives one among alternative responses". On computers with a random element, see A. M. Turing, "Computing Machinery and Intelligence", *Mind*, vol. 59 (1950), pp. 433–460.

of what has gone before except for canceling out curves that conflict with the data.[20]

A more sophisticated machine might make more use of the past. Let us suppose data have been fed to a machine, a choice of curve made, additional data supplied, a new choice made accordingly, and so on. The several choices may be regarded as steps in dealing with a single problem having as its cumulative data all those supplied from start to finish. Now the registers are cleared, data again are supplied, and the machine begins work on a new problem. Our present machine may, whenever it thus faces a new problem, look back to its encounters with earlier problems. After eliminating curves incompatible with the present data, it may find earlier problems with sets of data that properly include the present set, and proceed to cancel out

---

[20] My treatment throughout this section attempts only a simple schematic analysis of the process of supplementation. Variations and elaborations of all sorts may occur. The task may be to choose not one curve but a group of curves; e.g., if the ordinate at only one or a few abscissas is wanted, differences among curves that coincide at these abscissas can be ignored. Or, rather than canceling out curves not fitting the data, the machine may be asked to find among curves meeting some standard of smoothness the curve that comes nearest to fitting the data—though it miss some or even all points. Again, the response called for may not be to select or reject curves but to rate them according to relative probability. Also, the ways of taking cognizance of experience on past problems may be complicated and subtle. And where a scale of preference is involved it may be based upon simplicity of one sort or another, or upon more or different factors; and it may be fixed or variable. Finally, "points" and "curves" may be read more generally as "instances" and "hypotheses". None of this occludes the central issues above discussed.

every curve that conflicts with any of these more inclusive sets. It thus takes into account not only the immediate evidence, but evidence in past related cases.

Nevertheless, if the machine can handle enough curves, eliminations on the basis of present and past data will always leave a wide choice of alternatives—so wide, indeed, that no prediction concerning remaining points is excluded.[21] No matter for how many values of x the value of y is given, still for every remaining value m of x and every value n of y, at least one of the curves compatible with the data will pass through m,n. And this will hold true for any more comprehensive sets of data for past problems. Thus the less circumscribed the machine, the more often it must either consult a mandatory fixed scale of preference or resort to chance procedures. The erudite machine has to be either pigheaded or henheaded.

Both faults are corrected in a machine that can acquire habits. Appropriate inertia is required for maximum profit from experience. Suppose a machine to be so designed that in making any choice after its first it consults not only the data for the present and for past related problems but also the record of its own past choices. Among the curves remaining after deletions on the basis of all data, it selects or at least favors the one used most often before. And it sticks to a curve once chosen until forced to change by new data. Habit in effect establishes or modifies a preferential weighting; and a unique choice often results.

[21] Cf. *FFF*, pp. 72–81.

THE THEORY OF NOTATION

What I have been speaking of as 'the curves a machine can handle' constitute the inventory of responses it can make. No distinction has been drawn between those curves the machine has initially at its command and those, if any, that it can invent. A machine that can initially respond with straight lines only may be able, when fed three noncollinear points, to invent some new curve to accommodate these data. But this machine is as well described as one that, among all the curves it can handle, always chooses a straight line until forced by the data to make a different choice. The question what curves are 'there at the start' and what curves the machine 'generates' is thus displaced by the question what curves the machine can handle at all and how it chooses among them.

All these machines perform a task of supplementation, some by sheer guess, some by pure calculation, some by a mixture of the two. Some take no, some minimal, and some very extensive and complex account of the evidence. Those that take account of the evidence operate with curves that relate the given points to the rest. Some such machines can handle very few curves, some many, and some all possible curves in their universes. Certain machines, when confronted with open alternatives after all eliminations on the basis of the evidence, always make a unique choice by applying a preferential scale. Others, lacking such a fully automatic procedure, must sometimes resort to chance. Among these, some do and some do not take account of their past choices, in effect forming habits that perpetuate as far as possible chance decisions once made.

INDUCTIVE TRANSLATION

Questions concerning the nature of induction thrust themselves forward here.[22] Does supplementation become induction when account is taken of the evidence? Or not unless the evidence sometimes leaves open alternatives, so that a decision must be made by other means? Or only if for some such decisions a chance procedure is used? Giving an answer is perhaps less important than noting the several significant lines of demarcation. Again, what are the characteristics of the induction performed by human beings? Obviously, we can take account of the evidence in subtle and sophisticated ways. Obviously, also, we can handle any possible curve (or hypothesis). And on the whole we tend to persist in a choice so long as the evidence permits. But are we provided with a completely decisive preferential ordering among these curves, or must we sometimes resort to chance?

Our brief look at some ways of accomplishing message supplementation thus leads directly to the heart of active current controversy in epistemology. More to the immediate point of our present inquiry, though, is the disclosure of certain special features of the functioning of symbols not only in overt induction but also in such kindred processes as category detection and pattern perception: first, that evidence takes effect only through application of a general symbol (label or term or hypothesis) having an

[22] Cf. Marvin Minsky, "Steps toward Artificial Intelligence", in *Computers and Thought*, ed. E. A. Feigenbaum and J. Feldman (New York, McGraw-Hill Book Co., Inc., 1963), pp. 448–449. This article originally appeared in the special computer issue of the *Proceedings of the Institute of Radio Engineers*, 1961.

extension that properly includes the data; second, that the alternatives are primarily such general symbols, divergent in extension, rather than isolated particulars; and third, that pertinent time-and-trouble-saving habits can develop only through use of such symbols. Perhaps, indeed, these are earmarks of cognitive behavior in general.

10. Diagrams, Maps, and Models

Diagrams, whether they occur as the output of recording instruments or as adjuncts to expository texts or as operational guides, are often thought—because of their somewhat pictorial look and their contrast with their mathematical or verbal accompaniments—to be purely analog in type. Some, such as scale drawings for machinery, are indeed analog; but some others, such as diagrams of carbohydrates, are digital; and still others, such as ordinary road maps, are mixed.

The mere presence or absence of letters or figures does not make the difference. What matters with a diagram, as with the face of an instrument, is how we are to read it. For example, if figures on a barogram or seismogram indicate certain points the curve passes through, yet every point on the curve is a character with its own denotation, the diagram is purely analog, or *graphic*. But if the curve on a chart showing annual car production over a decade merely joins the several numbered points to emphasize the trend, the intermediate points on the curve are not characters of the scheme, and the diagram is purely digital. Nor is a diagram without alphabetical or arithmetical characters always analog. Many diagrams in topology, for example, need only have the right number of dots or junctures connected by lines in the right pattern, the size and location of the dots and the length and shape of the lines being irrelevant. Plainly, the dots and lines here function as characters in a notational language; and these diagrams, as well as most diagrams for electrical circuits, are purely digital. The more we are startled by this, because we think of such diagrams as rather schematized pictures, the more strongly are we reminded that the significant distinction between the digital or notational and the non-notational, including the analog, turns not upon some loose notion of analogy or resemblance but upon the grounded technical requirements for a notational language.

While scientists and philosophers have on the whole taken diagrams for granted, they have been forced to fret at some length about the nature and function of *models*.[23] Few terms are used in popular and scientific discourse more promiscuously than "model". A model is something to be admired or emulated, a pattern, a case in point, a type, a prototype, a specimen, a mock-up, a mathematical description—almost anything from a naked blonde to a quadratic equation—and may bear to what it models almost any relation of symbolization.

In many cases, a model is an exemplar or instance of what it models: the model citizen is a fine example of citizenship, the sculptor's model a sample of the human

---

[23] An exception to the first clause is Clerk Maxwell in the article on diagrams in the eleventh edition of the *Encyclopedia Britannica*, vol. 8 (Cambridge, England, Cambridge University Press, 1910), pp. 146–149. An example of the second clause is Boltzmann in the article on models in the same edition, vol. 18 (1911), pp. 638–640.

body, the fashion model a wearer, the model house a sample of the developer's offerings, and the model of a set of axioms is a compliant universe.

In other cases, the roles are reversed: the model denotes, or has as an instance, what it models. The car of a certain model belongs to a certain class. And a mathematical model is a formula that applies to the process or state or object modeled. What is modeled is the particular case that fits the description.

"Model" might well be dispensed with in all these cases in favor of less ambiguous and more informative terms, and reserved for cases where the symbol is neither an instance nor a verbal or mathematical description: the ship model, the miniature bulldozer, the architect's model of a campus, the wood or clay model of an automobile. None of these is a sample—a ship, a bulldozer, a campus, or a car; and none is a description in ordinary or mathematical language. Unlike samples, these models are denotative; unlike descriptions, they are nonverbal.[24] Models of this sort are in effect diagrams, often in more than two dimensions

---

[24] As noted in II,4, a sample may also take on the denotative role of and become coextensive with a label it exemplifies. The sample house may also function as a denotative model of houses in the development, including itself, and will then also exemplify itself as a label. It differs from the miniature model in the way that "polysyllabic" differs from "monosyllabic". Similarly, literal application of a schema may be a model for metaphorical applications, or may be at once a sample and a denotative model of all the applications. Incidentally, models are not, as sometimes supposed, necessarily metaphorical. Whether application of a model, as of any other label, is metaphorical depends upon whether the application is guided by an antecedently established literal application.

and with working parts; or in other words, diagrams are flat and static models. Like other diagrams, models may be digital or analog or mixed. Molecular models made of ping-pong balls and chopsticks are digital. A working model of a windmill may be analog. A scale model of a campus, with green papier-mâché for grass, pink cardboard for brick, plastic film for glass, etc., is analog with respect to spatial dimensions but digital with respect to materials. Perhaps the first step toward dispelling a good deal of confused romancing about models is to recognize that they can be treated as diagrams.

But how does a wiring diagram differ significantly, as a symbol, from verbal instructions, a road map from an aerial photograph, a ship model from a sculptural representation? I shall defer all such questions; for my purpose here has not been to study diagrams and models exhaustively but only to illustrate some of the concepts and principles developed in earlier sections.

The questions raised at the beginning of this chapter concerning notation in the arts have not been answered. Indeed, they have hardly been mentioned again. They had to be set aside while we examined some preliminary questions about notations and symbol systems in general. But the connection is less remote than it may seem; for a score, as I conceive it, is a character in a notational language, the compliants of a score are typically performances, and the compliance-class is a work. In the next chapter, I want to consider how some of our results apply to certain questions about the arts, and how some light may be reflected upon some other philosophical problems.

ce modius primus   Septimus ar monias

ic noscitur atq; secund.

tenet hanc Occa

ccipiatur tritus sic   uius aestam

Quartus et is

probatur   Quint

adest iste   Sextus

ic noscitur esse

Reverse

Page of manuscript, late eleventh century. Fol. 127 v. from
Lat. 7211, Bibliothèque Nationale, Paris.

V

SCORE, SKETCH, AND SCRIPT

You see no experiment can be repeated exactly. There will always be something different. . . . What it comes to when you say you repeat an experiment is that you repeat all the features of an experiment which a theory determines are relevant. In other words you repeat the experiment as an example of the theory.

Sir George Thomson*

1. Score

A score is a character in a notational system. Even in musical notation not every character is a score, but I count as a score every character that may have compliants. This excludes purely syncategorematic characters, for example, without requiring of a score either that it be a complete composition or that it be actually nonvacant. I have broadened the application of "score" to embrace characters of the sort described in any notational system,[1] not merely in musical notation. Similarly, I often call the compliants of such characters performances where these compliants are not by ordinary usage performed or even events at all; and

* In "Some Thoughts on Scientific Method", Lecture of May 2, 1963, printed in *Boston Studies in the Philosophy of Science*, vol. II (New York, Humanities Press, 1965), p. 85.

[1] Not, be it observed, "in any notational *scheme*". The usage here adopted counts only characters of notational *systems* as scores.

177

I often call the compliance-classes works, even when these classes are such—e.g., fortuitous aggregates of natural objects—as not to be works in any usual sense. All this I think may help to keep before us both the cardinal example of music and the more general principles illustrated.

A score, we found, defines a work but is a peculiar and privileged definition, without competitors. A class is uniquely determined by a score, as by an ordinary definition; but a score, unlike an ordinary definition, is also uniquely determined by each member of that class. Given the notational system and a performance of a score, the score is recoverable. Identity of work and of score is retained in any series of steps, each of them either from compliant performance to score-inscription, or from score-inscription to compliant performance, or from score-inscription to true copy. This is ensured by the fact, and only by the fact, that the language in which a score is written must be notational—must satisfy the five stated requirements. No inherent partitioning of the subject-matter is presumed; and performances of a work may vary widely and in many respects.

Redundancy, as noted earlier, is a common and minor violation of notationality. The net effect is that in a chain of the sort described, the score-inscriptions may not all be true copies of one another; yet all will be semantically equivalent—all performances will be of the same work. Work-preservation but not score-preservatioɪ is ensured; and insofar as work-preservation is paramount, and score-preservation incidental, redundancy is tolerable.

None of our usual natural languages is a notational system. Such *discursive languages* meet the two syntactic requirements but are exempt from the three semantic requirements. Accordingly, a definition or set of coextensive definitions is seldom uniquely determined by a member of the class defined. And as we have seen, ambiguity is not always to blame; a wheelbarrow belongs to many different compliance-classes of object-English—complies, that is, with many extensionally diverse descriptions, such as "wooden object", "wheeled vehicle", etc. In such a language there is no such thing as *the* definition, or set of equivalent definitions, that the given object satisfies. But in a notational system, or even a system that misses notationality only through redundancy, all scores for a given performance are coextensive—have all the same performances as compliants.

2. Music

So far, I have been discussing matters of general theory without examining closely any of the presumably notational systems actually used in the arts. Standard musical notation offers a familiar and at the same time a remarkable case. It is at once complex, serviceable, and—like Arabic numerical notation—common to the users of many different verbal languages. No alternative has gained any currency; and apparently no other culture, such as the Chinese or Indian, has developed any comparably effective musical notation over the centuries. The variety and vitality of recent rebellions against it testify to the authority it has acquired.[2]

---

[2] I do not say to its merits, aesthetic or otherwise; see the discussion of this point later in this section.

Ordinary musical notation has sometimes been thought to owe its origin to the introduction of keyboard instruments, with their separate keys and spaced tones; but the question just when either a true notation or a true keyboard instrument emerged is so elusive that the hypothesis hardly admits of any conclusive historical investigation. And the hypothesis is antecedently implausible; musical notation no more needed to wait upon invention of the clavichord than alphabetical notation needed to wait upon invention of the typewriter. Development of a notational scheme or system does not depend upon an intrinsic segregation of marks or objects into disjoint and differentiated sets, but is often achieved in the face of virtual continuity in both realms.

In some early mediaeval musical manuscripts, marks were placed higher or lower over syllables or words of a song to indicate pitch.[3] Only later did horizontal lines come to be added. At first these lines may have functioned as mere guides for judging absolute position, like the graduation-marks on a therometer taken as an analog in-

---

[3] See the frontispiece to this chapter. According to Carl Parrish, *The Notation of Medieval Music* (New York, W. W. Norton & Co., Inc., 1957), p. 9, this system "is called *diastematic* from the Greek word for 'interval'. In this writing neumes are carefully 'heighted', that is, placed at various distances from an imaginary line representing a given pitch, according to their relationship to that line. Certain schools of neume notation display this feature even in their earliest manuscripts. . . . About the end of the tenth century the imaginary line about which diastematic neumes were placed became a real one. At first it was a dry line scratched on the parchment, an idea probably suggested by the use of the guidelines on which the text was written".

strument. When the lines and the spaces between them become characters of the system, with placement of a syllable or note-sign serving only to pick out one of these characters, elements of a genuine notation emerge. However, I am primarily concerned here not with origins or development but with how fully the language of musical scores qualifies as a truly notational system.

That the syntactic requirements are in general met is quite clear. A note-mark may, indeed, be so placed that we are in doubt about whether it belongs to one note-character or another, but in no case does it belong to both. Ostensible note-marks do not count as inscriptions in the system unless and until they are determined to belong to one character rather than to any other. Most characters of a musical score, whether numerals or letters or neither, are syntactically disjoint and differentiated. The symbol scheme is thus substantially notational, and the language of scores truly a language. But is this language a notational system? Does it satisfy the semantic requirements?

If we consider piano scores alone, the language is highly redundant since, for example, the same sound-events comply with the characters for c-sharp, d-flat, e-triple-flat, b-double-sharp, and so on [4]; but redundancy, as we have seen, is not altogether fatal. A more crucial question arises when we consider scores for other instruments as well. In a violin score the characters for c-sharp and d-flat have no

---

[4] I oversimplify here by ignoring features other than pitch, but the central point is unaffected. The redundancy noted above will call for further consideration in another connection.

compliants in common.[5] Now if two characters thus have some compliants jointly (in piano scores) and others severally, the two compliance-classes properly intersect, flagrantly violating the requirement of semantic disjointness. What this account misses, though, is that since every performance is on one instrument or another, each of the two characters can be considered a vacant atomic character that combines with different specifications of instrument to form different prime characters. The compliance-classes of the two resultant prime characters occurring in piano scores are identical; the compliance-classes of the two resultant prime characters occurring in violin scores are disjoint. Neither pair nor the pair of atomic vacant characters nor the set of all six characters violates the rule of semantic disjointness by more than the redundancy mentioned.

If we suppose the series of whole note, half-note, quarter-note, eighth-note, etc., to be continued without end, the semantic requirement of finite differentiation will be violated. For then by tying note-signs together we can construct characters for notes differing in duration by less than any given fraction of a beat. Hence no sounding of a note could be determined to comply with at most one character. Now of course in any given score or corpus of

[5] This may be disputed. I am told that a tone of, say, 333 vibrations per second is accepted for either character. But we may regard such a tone either as actually compliant with both characters or (like the missing of one note) as merely within tolerable limits of deviation in practice. For purposes of illustrating a general point, I choose the latter interpretation here. A more relational notation is still compatible with notationality.

scores, the number of note-signs, and of flags on any of them, is finite. But there must furthermore be a tacit or express limit on the number of flags permitted by the system at all; otherwise recovery of score from performance will not be even theoretically possible, identity of work from performance to performance will not be ensured, and the primary purpose of a notational system will not be served. Theoretically, any limit would do. Tradition seems to set it for the present at five flags—the 1/128 note.

The main corpus of peculiarly musical characters of the system thus appears on the whole to meet the semantic as well as the syntactic requirements for a notation. The same cannot be said for all the numerical and alphabetical characters that also occur in scores.

First, some compositions are written with a 'figured bass' or 'continuo', allowing performers certain options. Now so long as such scores determine comparatively broad but still mutually disjoint classes of performances,[6] they cause no trouble; what counts is not specificity but separateness. But a system that permits alternative use of figured-bass and specific notation, without rigidly prescribing the choice in every case, materially violates the conditions upon notational systems; for the compliance-classes of some of its characters are properly included in the compliance-classes of other, more general characters. Two score-inscriptions, one in figured-bass and the other

---

[6] The question whether these compliance-classes are in fact disjoint can be answered only by careful examination of the notation in use and some delicate decisions concerning its interpretation.

in specific notation, even though they have some common compliant performance, will not thereby be semantically equivalent; and two performances complying with the former may severally comply with two specific scores that have no compliant in common. The comprehensive language of musical scores, insofar as it offers free choice between figured-bass and specific notation, is thus not truly notational. Rather, it comprises two notational subsystems; and the one in use must be designated and adhered to if identification of work from performance to performance is to be ensured.

Much the same can be said concerning the free cadenza. The performer, again, is given wide scope; and scores providing for free cadenzas have compliance-classes that properly include those of other scores with their solo passages all specified note by note. Unless there is a way of determining in every case whether a solo passage is to be fully specified or indicated as a free cadenza, we must again recognize that the language of musical scores is not purely notational but divides into notational subsystems.

Trouble of a different sort arises from the verbal notation used for the tempo of a movement. That the words come from ordinary object-language does not of itself matter. "Notational" does not imply "nonverbal"; and not every selection of characters, along with their compliance-classes, from a discursive language violates the conditions for notationality. What matters is whether the borrowed vocabulary meets the semantic requirements. Now just what is the vocabulary of tempo? It contains not only the more common terms like "allegro", "andante", and "adagio", but indefinitely many others like the following, taken from a few programs of chamber music [7]: *presto, allegro vivace, allegro assai, allegro spiritoso, allegro molto, allegro non troppo, allegro moderato, poco allegretto, allegretto quasi-minuetto, minuetto, minuetto con un poco di moto, rondo alla Pollaca, andantino mosso, andantino grazioso, fantasia, affetuoso e sostenuto, moderato e amabile.* Apparently almost any words may be used to indicate pace and mood. Even if unambiguity were miraculously preserved, semantic disjointness would not be. And since a tempo may be prescribed as fast, or as slow, or as between fast and slow, or as between fast and between-fast-and-slow, and so on without limit, semantic differentiation goes by the board, too.

Thus the verbal language of tempos is not notational. The tempo words cannot be integral parts of a score insofar as the score serves the function of identifying a work from performance to performance. No departure from the indicated tempo disqualifies a performance as an instance —however wretched—of the work defined by the score. For these tempo specifications cannot be accounted integral parts of the defining score, but are rather auxiliary directions whose observance or nonobservance affects the quality of a performance but not the identity of the work. On the other hand, metronomic specifications of tempo do, under obvious restrictions and under a system univer-

[7] Chosen casually from programs of works played at the Marlboro Music Festival, Marlboro, Vermont, during six weeks in the summer of 1961.

sally requiring them, qualify as notational and may be taken as belonging to the score as such.

I have been able to discuss here, rather sketchily, only a few salient samples of relevant questions concerning the standard language of musical scores. The results suggest, however, that it comes as near to meeting the theoretical requirements for notationality as might reasonably be expected of any traditional system in constant actual use, and that the excisions and revisions needed to correct any infractions are rather plain and local. After all, one hardly expects chemical purity outside the laboratory.

Since complete compliance with the score is the only requirement for a genuine instance of a work, the most miserable performance without actual mistakes does count as such an instance, while the most brilliant performance with a single wrong note does not. Could we not bring our theoretical vocabulary into better agreement with common practice and common sense by allowing some limited degree of deviation in performances admitted as instances of a work? The practicing musician or composer usually bristles at the idea that a performance with one wrong note is not a performance of the given work at all; and ordinary usage surely sanctions overlooking a few wrong notes. But this is one of those cases where ordinary usage gets us quickly into trouble. The innocent-seeming principle that performances differing by just one note are instances of the same work risks the consequence—in view of the transitivity of identity—that all performances whatsoever are of the same work. If we allow the least deviation, all assurance of work-preservation and score-preservation is lost; for by a series of one-note errors of omission, addition, and modification, we can go all the way from Beethoven's *Fifth Symphony* to *Three Blind Mice*. Thus while a score may leave unspecified many features of a performance, and allow for considerable variation in others within prescribed limits, full compliance with the specifications given is categorically required. This is not to say that the exigencies that dictate our technical discourse need govern our everyday speech. I am no more recommending that in ordinary discourse we refuse to say that a pianist who misses a note has performed a Chopin Polonaise than that we refuse to call a whale a fish, the earth spherical, or a grayish-pink human white.

The overwhelming monopoly long held by standard musical notation has inevitably inspired rebellion and alternative proposals. Composers complain variously that scores in this notation prescribe too few features or too many or the wrong ones, or prescribe the right ones too precisely or not precisely enough. Revolution here as elsewhere may aim at more or at less or at different control of the means of production.

One simple system devised by John Cage is roughly as follows (see Figure 11): dots, for single sounds, are placed within a rectangle; across the rectangle, at varying angles and perhaps intersecting, run five straight lines for (severally) frequency, duration, timbre, amplitude, and succession. The significant factors determining the sounds indicated by a dot are the perpendicular distances from the

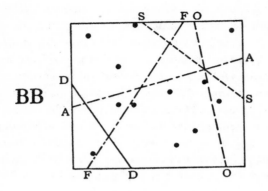

Figure 11

dot to these lines.[8] This system is not notational; for without some stipulation of minimal significant units of angle and distance, syntactic differentiation is wanting. So long as no limit is set upon the smallness of the difference in position that makes a difference in character, no measurement can ever determine that any mark belongs to one character rather than to any number of others. Similarly, under this system, no measurement can ever determine that a performance complies with one mark rather than others. Furthermore, depending upon just how the symbols are interpreted, syntactic and semantic disjointness may be lacking. The point is not that a work is less rigidly prescribed than by a standard score; for the character-classes and the

[8] See *Concert for Piano and Orchestra, Solo for Piano* (New York, Henmar Press, Inc., 1960), p. 53, figure BB. The figure, which has been redrawn, is reproduced here by permission of the publisher.

compliance-classes of a notational system may be of any size so long as they are disjoint and differentiated. Under the proposed system there are no disjoint and differentiated characters or compliance-classes, no notation, no language, no scores.

The objection may be raised that the lack of syntactic differentiation here hardly matters if we have the original drawing and photographic means of reproducing it within any desired or consequential degree of accuracy. But however small the inaccuracy of reproduction, a chain of successive reproductions of reproductions can result in departing to any degree from the original. True enough, we can detect significant deviation by direct comparison with the original (if it is available); yet for two significantly different originals there may be a third (or a copy) that does not differ significantly from either. To arrive at a notation here calls not only for a limit upon significant deviation but also for a means of ensuring disjointness of characters.

Now I am by no means pronouncing upon whether adoption of a system like that described might nevertheless be a good idea. I am neither qualified nor called upon to make such a judgment. I am simply pointing out that much more is involved than a mere shift from one notational system to another. Nor am I quibbling about the proper use of such words as "notation", "score", and "work". That matters little more than the proper use of a fork. What does matter is that the system in question furnishes no means of identifying a work from performance to performance or even of a character from mark to mark. Nothing can be determined to be a true copy of Cage's autograph diagram or to be a performance of it. There are only copies *after* and performances *after* that unique object as there are only drawings and paintings after a sketch. The same, of course, may be said of the mediaeval manuscript shown in the frontispiece to this chapter; sometimes revolution is retrogression.

An extreme spirit of *laissez faire* has led some composers to use systems that restrict only slightly the performer's freedom to play what and as he pleases. Such latitude is not incompatible with notationality; even a system with only two characters, one having as compliants all piano performances beginning with a middle c, and the other having as compliants all other performances, would be notational—though for this system there could be only two different works. But, of course, systems with characters having wide ranges of application often lack semantic disjointness.

At the opposite extreme, some composers of electronic music, with continuous sound-sources and means of activation, and with the human performer dispensable in favor of mechanical devices, seek to eliminate all latitude in performance and achieve 'exact control'.[9] But except where

[9] Roger Sessions, in a passage just preceding the paragraph from which the quotation heading Chapter IV is taken, writes that electronic media make possible "the exact control of all musical elements. . . . Every moment of music not only can but must be the result of the minutest calculation, and the composer for the first time has the whole world of sound at his disposal"; then he proceeds to question the musical importance of this approach. Peter Yates, in "The Proof of the Notation", *Arts and Architecture*, vol. 82 (1966), p. 36, points out that "Even a performance by electronic means will vary with the equipment and acoustics".

mere counting is involved, absolutely precise prescription cannot be accomplished by any notational system; differentiation requires gaps that destroy continuity. With a decimal system, for example, absolute precision would require writing out each specification endlessly; stopping at any finite number of decimal places results in some inaccuracy, however slight, that could accumulate in a long enough chain to any amount. For exact control, the symbol system would have to be both syntactically and semantically dense—an analog or graphic system; then any imprecision would arise from mechanical or human errors or limitations rather than from the symbol system. But then, also, we have no notation or scores, and ironically the demand for absolute and inflexible control results in purely autographic works.

Many of the symbol systems developed by modern composers have been described, illustrated, and classified by Erhardt Karkoschka.[10] His classification, differently motivated from ours, recognizes four basic types of system:

(1) Precise Notation (*Präzise Notation*)—where, for example, every note is named.
(2) Range Notation (*Rahmenotation*)—where, for example, only the limits of ranges of notes are set.
(3) Suggestive Notation (*Hinweisende Notation*)—where at most relations of notes, or approximate limits of ranges, are specified.
(4) Musical Graphics.

---

[10] In *Das Schriftsbild der Neuen Musik* (Celle, Herman Moeck, 1966), pp. 19ff. My discussion of this searching work is brief and inadequate.

Obviously, a system of either of the first two kinds may or may not qualify as notational in my terminology. Systems of the third kind seem in general to be non-notational; they include, for example, the usual verbal tempo descriptions. But a system prescribing only relations between notes—such as that one is twice as loud or an octave below the preceding note—seems also to belong to the third class and could be notational. The system used for Gregorian chant may have been of this sort. Of his first three classes, Karkoschka writes (p. 80): "A work falls in the three spheres of precise notation, range notation, and suggestive notation if it has the usual coordinate system of space and time as basis, is more sign than sketch, and is essentially linear." The fourth class, musical graphics, apparently consists mainly of analog systems, lacking both syntactic and semantic articulation—that is, of non-notational, nonlinguistic systems that provide diagrams or sketches rather than scores or descriptions.

3. Sketch

Because a painter's sketch, like a composer's score, may be used as a working guide, the crucial difference in their status might go unnoticed. The sketch, unlike the score, is not in a language or notation at all, but in a system without either syntactic or semantic differentiation. And while the Cage system described takes certain relationships of dot to line as the only pertinent ones, none among the pictorial properties of a sketch can be dismissed as irrelevant. But in neither case can anything be determined to belong to or to comply with at most one character. Thus, whereas a true score picks out a class of performances that are the equal and only instances of a musical work, a sketch does not determine a class of objects that are the equal and only instances of a work of painting. Unlike the score, the sketch does not define a work, in the strong sense of "define" explained earlier, but rather *is* one.

Now this is not to deny that a notational system might be established such that sketches belong to its characters. Obviously sketches and also paintings can be sorted into disjoint and differentiated classes in any of various ways; and any of a multitude of correlations can be set up. But quite as obviously, to have two realms that can be so sorted and correlated is not yet to have a system. Only when custom or express stipulation actually effects or selects a classification of each realm and a correlation of the two do we have a system. Such a selection has already been made in the case of standard musical notation, but not in the case of sketches. No pictorial respects are distinguished as those in which a sketch must match another to be its equivalent, or a painting match a sketch to be an instance of what the sketch defines. And no magnitude of difference in any respect is set as the threshhold of significance. Differences of all kinds and degrees, measurable or not, are on equal footing. Hence no classes of sketches are picked out as the characters, and no classes of pictures as the compliance-classes, of a notational system.

In short, the sketch—as a sketch—differs from the score

not in functioning as a character in a language of a different kind but in not functioning as a character in a *language* at all.[11] The notational language of musical scores has no parallel in a language (notational or not) of sketches.

4. Painting

That we have ready at hand no notational system for painting does not settle the question whether such a system is possible. Taken at its face value, the question can be answered with an unhesitating but trivial *yes*. For examples of such notational languages are easily constructed. A library-like decimal system assigning a numeral to each painting according to time and place of production would meet all five requirements. Far afield is the objection that no one can tell by inspection, without further information, whether a given painting complies with a given numeral; for likewise no one can tell by inspection, *without further information*, whether a given performance complies with a musical score. One has to be able to interpret the score as one has to be able to interpret the numeral; and to know how to interpret a character is to know what complies with it.

The compliance-classes for the language just described will indeed be unit-classes, so that identification of a work from instance to instance will always be from sole instance to same sole instance, but there are no requirements upon

---

[11] Of course, nothing prevents a given mark from functioning as an inscription in a notation (or in several different notations) and also as a sketch in a nonlinguistic system (or in several such systems).

the size of the compliance-classes of a notational system. And the uniqueness of instance in painting is irrelevant here since exactly the same question about the possibility of a notational system arises for etching, and is to be answered in the same way. If impressions are assigned numerals according to the plate printed from, the compliance-class of a numeral will usually have many members. Indeed, nothing precludes taking each plate itself as the unique inscription of a character having its impressions as its compliants. Hence for painting and etching alike, notational languages are readily devised.

Yet, clearly, this straight-faced answer to the literal question asked misses the main point. For the question of real interest here is whether by means of a notational system the work of painting or etching can be freed of dependence upon a particular author or upon a place or date or means of production. Is it theoretically possible to write a score so defining a work of painting or etching that objects produced by others, before or since the usually designated original or originals, and by other means (than, e.g., the 'original' plate) may comply with the score and qualify as equal instances of the work? In short, could institution of a notational system transform painting or etching from an autographic into an allographic art?

Some reasons that have been given for a negative answer are plainly beside the point. That a visual work is more complex and subtle than a musical performance would— even if true—not matter. For a score need not—indeed cannot—specify all aspects of the compliants nor even every degree of difference in any aspect; a score, as in figured-bass or free-cadenza notation, may be summary in the extreme. Nor does the difficulty of making perfect reproductions of a painting have anything to do with confinement of the work to the unique original.[12] The performances of the most specific score are by no means exact duplicates of one another, but vary widely and in many ways. A moderately good copy and the original painting resemble each other more closely than do performances of a Bach suite by Piatigorsky and Casals.

Yet there are constraints. Although a notational system may pick out any set of disjoint and finitely differentiated classes in any realm as compliance-classes, not every compliance-class of every such system counts as a work. Standard musical notation might be reinterpreted so that its compliance-classes cut wildly across the standard ones or even contain no musical performances at all. Or a notational system might classify pictures according to size or shape. But in none of these cases does a compliance-class any more constitute a work than the animals in a zoo form a species, or the performances of a musical composition make up a society. Whether the compliance-classes for a system are works (or societies) depends partly upon their relationship to the classes accounted works (or societies) in antecedent practice.

Special care must be taken here. While it would be quite

---

[12] Widespread acceptance of this easy and inapt explanation has inhibited efforts toward real understanding of the matter. Philosophers of art are not immune from the error; see, for example, Joseph Margolis, "The Identity of a Work of Art", *Mind*, vol. 68 (1959), p. 50.

wrong to suppose that a class becomes a work by being assigned a character in a notational system, it would also be quite wrong to suppose that no class is a work unless it has been antecedently considered so. On the one hand, the antecedent classification stands as license and touchstone for a notational system; only in reference to this classification can there be a charge of material error or a claim of material correctness. On the other hand, the antecedent classification is normally partial and provisional. It submits only sample classes, each only by samples. Adoption of a notational language thus effects a double projection: from the samples of the several classes to the complete classes, and from the sample classes to the complete classification of the field of reference. This involves a choice among alternatives; and some actual departures from the antecedent classification may be made for the sake of better systematization. In sum, the problem of developing a notational system for an art like music amounted to the problem of arriving at a real definition of the notion of a musical work.

Where a pertinent antecedent classification is lacking or is flouted, a notational language effects only an arbitrary, nominal definition of "work", as if it were a word newly coined. With no prototype, or no recognition of one, there are no material grounds for choosing one systematization rather than any other. But in the case of painting, a work is antecedently identified with (the unit-class of) an individual picture; and in the case of etching, with the class of impressions printed from an individual plate. Now the question is whether by application of a notational system works of painting or etching could legitimately be identified with quite different classes. This would call not just for such minor adjustments as occur in any systematization but for a drastic overhaul that would lump together in each compliance-class many antecedently different works. A notational system effecting such a reclassification may of course be applied at will; but scores in it will not constitute real definitions of works of painting. To repudiate the antecedent classification is to disenable the only authority competent to issue the needed license.

Thus the answer to the significant question about a notational system for painting is *no*. We can devise a notational system that will provide, for works of painting and etching, real definitions that depend upon history of production. We can devise a notational system that will provide purely arbitrary nominal definitions that do not depend upon history of production. But we cannot devise a notational system that will provide, for such works, definitions that are both real (consonant with antecedent practice) and independent of history of production.

In sum, an established art becomes allographic only when the classification of objects or events into works is legitimately projected from an antecedent classification and is fully defined, independently of history of production, in terms of a notational system. Both authority and means are required; a suitable antecedent classification provides the one, a suitable notational system the other. Without the means, the authority is unexercised; without the authority, the means are footless.

5. Script

A script, unlike a sketch, is a character in a notational scheme and in a language but, unlike a score, is not in a notational system. The syntactic but not all the semantic requirements are met. "Script" here is thus not confined to cursive inscriptions or to the work of playwrights and film writers. In general, the characters of natural and of most technical languages are scripts; for even if ambiguity is avoided, the compliance-classes of such a language are seldom either disjoint or differentiated from one another.

While most scripts are verbal, notationality obviously does not turn upon the look of marks. We do not arrive at a notational system if we substitute a numeral for each word of English.[13] And we do not sacrifice notationality —although we surely jettison practicality—if we translate standard musical notation into a sublanguage of English in such a way that the vocabulary of admitted words meets our five requirements.

One might suppose that scripts but not scores can assert or denote. But we have already seen that means of effecting assertion (or question or command) can be added to or subtracted from a system without affecting notational-

---

[13] Lexicographical order might be taken as the basis for assigning numerals to words. But if we want to assign a numeral to *every string of letters*, and we place no limit on the length of a string, lexicographical ordering becomes astoundingly complex. However, numerals may be assigned to all such strings on the basis of the different and very simple ordering that begins with lexicographical ordering of all one-letter strings, proceeds to lexicographical ordering of all two-letter strings, and so on. See IV, note 17.

ity; and the idea that scores do not denote seems no better founded. Offhand, indeed, the relation between a term and what it denotes appears quite different from that between a score and its performances or between a letter and its utterances; but no very clear principle seems to underlie this distinction. The criteria that distinguish notational systems from other languages are in terms of interrelationships among compliance-classes, and provide no good grounds for refusing to say that a character in a language of either sort denotes what complies with it.[14]

Even less can be said for the notion that while we need only know how to recognize a performance of a musical score or an utterance of a phonetic score, we have to understand a script. In both cases, we have to know how to determine what complies with the character. Where a language has few prime characters and fairly simple principles of compliance, so that confident and almost automatic use is acquired rather easily, we tend to regard the language as an instrument we operate. Where the prime characters are many and the principles of compliance are complex, so that interpretation of a character often calls for some deliberation, we tend to speak of having to understand the language. But this difference in complexity, besides being a matter of degree, does not at all coincide with

[14] This is not to say that everything a symbol refers to complies with it; exemplification, though a mode of reference, does not constitute compliance. Also we shall see below (section 7) that the utterances and inscriptions of a language may alternatively, and often happily, be construed as equally instances of visual-auditory characters.

the distinction between notational systems and other languages. For a notational system may have a denumerable infinity of prime characters and an intricate compliance-relation, while a discursive language may have only two characters—say the words "red" and "square", with red things and square things as their compliants.

A script, then, differs from a score not in being verbal or declarative or denotational or in requiring special understanding, but simply in being a character in a language that is either ambiguous or lacks semantic disjointness or differentiation. But this prosaic distinction is more consequential than might appear, both in ways already observed and in its bearing upon some currently touchy philosophical questions.

6. Projectibility, Synonymy, Analyticity

To learn and use any language is to resolve problems of projection. On the basis of sample inscriptions of a character we must decide whether other marks, as they appear, belong to that character; and on the basis of sample compliants of a character, we must decide whether other objects comply. Notational and discursive languages are alike in this respect.

With discursive languages, further and major projective decisions have to be made. Even after all questions about what marks belong to what characters and about what objects belong to what compliance-classes have been settled, still an object often complies with several characters.

In object-English, for example, no object or set of objects complies with just one predicate. All green objects examined to date comply with the character "green object", but all comply equally with "green object examined to date or kangaroo", and with indefinitely many other predicates. Virtually any class that contains all green objects examined to date is the compliance-class of some expression in this language. More generally, the objects in any given selection comply with some English description that has as its other compliants any other given objects. Thus projection from given cases calls for a choice among countless alternatives; and the making of such choices pervades all learning.[15]

Yet no such questions arise when we are using a notational system. Here nothing is a sample of more than one compliance-class; nothing complies with two characters that are not coextensive. So no choice remains except perhaps, where redundancy is permitted, between coextensive labels; projection even from single sample to compliance-class is uniquely determined. What has happened, in effect, is that the decisions have already been taken in adopting the system. We saw earlier that selection and

[15] What constitutes the grounds for choice here is a moot question. Scientists and metaphysicians are wont to posit an ontological difference between 'natural kinds' and other classes. Philosophers often hold that members of a favored class share some real attribute or essence, or bear some absolute resemblance to each other. I think the distinction depends rather upon linguistic habit. For a detailed discussion of the problem of projectibility, see *FFF*.

application of a notational system resolves problems of projection on two levels: from partial to complete compliance-classes, and from partial to complete set of compliance-classes. Hence so long as we use that system, we are free of the major problems of projectibility.

Of course, part of a performance no more determines the rest than does part of an object. Hearing the first notes of a composition no more tells us what follows than seeing part of an object tells us what lies beyond our view. The difference is that under a notational system one complete performance (whether of a single prime character or of the entire score of a symphony) uniquely determines character and compliance-class, while under a discursive language one complete object or event complying with a character does not uniquely determine character or compliance-class.

Furthermore a notational system, unlike a discursive language, is accordingly untroubled by any distinction in nobility among different ways of classifying an object. An object cannot be assigned by one character of the system to a natural or genuine kind and by another to a random or artificial collection. All labels for an object have the same compliance-class. We cannot, in standard musical notation for example, specify merely that a note is a quarter-note regardless of pitch or merely that it is a middle c regardless of duration. We have no label for all quarter-notes or for all middle c's; detached note-signs and empty staff lines must be taken as vacant characters if notationality is to be preserved. All the properties of a given object that are specifiable in a given notational system are thus coextensive.

The distinction between real and nominal defining still stands, as is illustrated by the difference between writing a score for a work already extant in performance and composing a new work. Once the language is given, a score or class of coextensive scores is in the first case uniquely determined by a performance, and a class of performances is in the second case uniquely determined by a score. But in both cases, all scores for a performance assign it to the same compliance-class: nothing is a performance of more than a single work. Where two works are performed in succession the resultant event, though it contains performances of each of the two, is itself a performance of neither but of the conjoint score.

That all scores for a performance are coextensive does not imply that all are synonymous. Two coextensive characters, c_1 and c_2, are not synonymous unless every two parallel compounds of them are also coextensive. That is, if replacement of c_1 or c_2 by the other in some compound character k_1 yields a character k_2 with an extension different from that of k_1, then c_1 and c_2 may on good grounds be said to differ in meaning.[16] Furthermore, where two terms thus differ in meaning, even coextensive parallel compounds of them may be considered, derivatively, to differ in meaning. We noticed earlier that a c-sharp-sign and a d-flat-sign (equal in indicated duration, etc.) as they occur in piano scores have the same compliance-class of sounds, but that

[16] The criterion of difference in meaning here employed is that set forth in my papers "On Likeness of Meaning" and "On Some Dif-

since the effect of adding the natural-sign to these characters is to negate the sharp-sign and the flat-sign alike, the
compliance-class for the c-sharp-natural-sign [17] consists of
c-sounds and is disjoint from the compliance-class, consisting of *d*-sounds, for the *d*-flat-natural-sign. Thus the c-
sharp-sign and the *d*-flat-sign, even though coextensive, are
not synonymous; and neither are two scores, even if coextensive, that are parallel compounds of these characters.[18]

ferences About Meaning" (cited in I, note 19). The *primary* extension
of a character consists of what that character denotes; a *secondary*
extension consists of what some compound of that character denotes.
Two characters differ in meaning if they differ in primary extension
or in any of their parallel secondary extensions. As applied to natural
languages, where there is great freedom in generating compounds, this
criterion tends to give the result that every two terms differ in
meaning. No such result follows for more restricted languages; and
indeed for these the criterion may need to be strengthened by providing further that characters differ in meaning if they are parallel
compounds of terms that differ either in primary or in parallel
secondary extension.

[17] The characters here in question comprise a note-sign, a sharp-sign
or flat-sign (perhaps from the signature), and a natural-sign that
neutralizes the sharp-sign or flat-sign. The order of precedence of
the note-sign and the sharp-sign or flat-sign makes no difference; but
a natural-sign cancels all and only the sharp-signs or flat-signs that
precede it and are (immediately or remotely) associated with the
note-sign. To modify a c-double-sharp to a c-sharp, we must suffix a
natural-sign and then another sharp-sign, so that the unabbreviated
result is a c-sharp-sharp-natural-sharp-sign.

[18] All never-performed scores have the same (i.e., no) performances
as compliants. They are scores for 'different works' in the oblique
sense that pictures of unicorns and pictures of centaurs are pictures of
different things. In neither case is there a difference in primary extension. The score for Jones's never-performed Symphony #9 and
the score for his never-performed Piano Concerto #3 are strictly

SCORE, SKETCH, AND SCRIPT

Wherever there are coextensive nonsynonymous characters, a question may arise concerning principles of preference among them in any given context. Although "rational animal" and "featherless biped" be coextensive, still "All men are rational animals" is said—upon rather obscure grounds—to be analytic, and "All men are featherless bipeds" to be synthetic. How do matters stand in a system that is notational except for containing some coextensive characters? Musicians tell us that in a traditional piano score the usual rules of composition unequivocally decide whether a c-sharp-sign or a d-flat-sign should occur. Although no difference in performance can result, the wrong choice seems to violate a rule of grammatical etiquette comparable to that governing, say, the use in English of the prefixes "un" and "in". Indeed, we might say that using a c-sharp-sign where a d-flat-sign belongs is like saying that such a choice is untolerable (or inbearable).

A more substantive consideration might be found in the relation of a work to its siblings for other instruments. As we have seen, specification of instrument is an integral part of any true score in standard musical notation; and a piano work and the violin version of it, for example, count strictly as different works. Nevertheless, certain violin performances rather than others are accepted as performances of the violin version of the piano work. Let us sup-

---

just the Jones-Symphony-#9-score and the Jones-Piano-Concerto-#3-score. Replacement of a character in the Jones-Symphony-#9-score will result in the Jones-Symphony-#9-score only if the replaced and replacing characters are coextensive and furthermore, in the way explained above, synonymous.

pose that for a given piano work the violin performances so recognized have a c-sharp and not a *d*-flat at a given place. The score for the violin version of the piano work must then have at that place a c-sharp-sign and not a *d*-flat-sign. This would provide grounds for choosing the c-sharp-sign in the piano score itself; the piano work might be said to have the c-sharp analytically in that in versions of the work for other instruments, where the c-sharp-sign and the *d*-flat-sign are not coextensive, a c-sharp is mandatory.

How close such a criterion comes to the usual notion of analyticity is hard to say, since that notion is so hopelessly confused. But musical notation seems to offer so much less opportunity than does English for befuddlement over analyticity that some philosophers might do well to stop writing and start composing.

7. Literary Arts

The text of a poem or novel or biography is a character in a notational scheme. As a phonetic character, with utterances as compliants, it belongs to an approximately notational system.[19] As a character with objects as compliants, it belongs to a discursive language.

Since in the latter case the compliance-classes are not disjoint or differentiated, texts are not scores but scripts. If compliance-classes of texts constituted works, then in some cases whether an object belongs to a given work

---

[19] The approximation will not be very close in English, with its wealth of homonyms, inconstancies, etc., but may be fairly close in a language like Spanish.

would be theoretically indeterminable, and in some cases an object would be an instance of several works. But obviously works of literature are not compliance-classes of texts. The Civil War is not literature; and two histories of it are different works.

Nor can the work of literature be identified as the class of utterances compliant with the text taken as a phonetic character. For even though the text be a true score, with an exclusive disjoint and differentiated compliance-class, an utterance obviously has no better title to be considered an instance of the work than does an inscription of the text. Utterances are not the end-products as are performances in music. Moreover, the utterances themselves might equally well be considered either as coextensive with inscriptions of the text or as belonging to a converse-phonetic language and having the inscriptions as compliants. Or since compliance is not always asymmetrical, utterances and inscriptions could be considered as having each other as their compliants. Or we might take written and spoken English say, as separate and parallel languages. A character of the one consists of inscriptions, a character of the other consists of utterances, while "character of English" can be taken either way if no restrictions are imposed by the context. But perhaps the simplest course is to consider a character of English to have utterances and inscriptions alike as members. This merely extends in a convenient and appropriate way the practice of counting widely varying marks as members of a single character. Syntactic disjointness—required of a notational scheme and hence of any language, not merely of a notational system—

will have to be preserved by refusing to accept any utterance as belonging to two different characters. Just as among certain matching letter-inscriptions some belong to the first letter of the alphabet while some belong to the fourth, so among utterances consisting of a hard-*g*-sound followed by a long-*a*-sound followed by a *t*-sound some will belong to the same character as inscriptions of "gate" while some will belong to the same character as inscriptions of "gait".

A literary work, then, is not the compliance-class of a text but the text or script itself. All and only inscriptions and utterances of the text are instances of the work; and identification of the work from instance to instance is ensured by the fact that the text is a character in a notational scheme—in a vocabulary of syntactically disjoint and differentiated symbols. Even replacement of a character in a text by another synonymous character (if any can be found in a discursive language) yields a different work. Yet the work is the text not as an isolated class of marks and utterances but as a character in a language. The same class as a character in another language is another work, and a translation of a work is not an instance of that work. Both identity of language and syntactic identity within the language are necessary conditions for identity of a literary work.

Obviously I am not concerned with what distinguishes some scripts as 'truly literary' works. Nevertheless, equating a poem with its text may arouse some protest, on the ground that the more immediate or intrinsic properties of classes of inscriptions and utterances hardly coincide with the aesthetically important properties of the poem. But in the first place, defining literary works no more calls for setting forth all their significant aesthetic properties than defining metals calls for setting forth all their significant chemical properties. In the second place, immediacy is a suspect notion and aesthetic relevance a subtle one; and no end of confusion has arisen from association of the two. To identify the literary work with a script is not to isolate and dessicate it but to recognize it as a denotative and expressive symbol that reaches beyond itself along all sorts of short and long referential paths.

We have seen that a musical score is in a notation and defines a work; that a sketch or picture is not in a notation but is itself a work; and that a literary script is both in a notation and is itself a work. Thus in the different arts a work is differently localized. In painting, the work is an individual object; and in etching, a class of objects. In music, the work is the class of performances compliant with a character. In literature, the work is the character itself. And in calligraphy, we may add, the work is an individual inscription.[20]

In the drama, as in music, the work is a compliance-class of performances. The text of a play, however, is a composite of score and script. The dialogue is in a virtually notational system, with utterances as its compliants. This part of the text is a score; and performances compliant with it

[20] The much discussed question whether a work of art is a symbol thus seems to me particularly fruitless. Not only may a work, depending upon the art, be an object or a class of objects or a character in a language or an inscription, but whichever it is it may in various ways symbolize other things.

constitute the work. The stage directions, descriptions of scenery, etc., are scripts in a language that meets none of the semantic requirements for notationality; and a performance does not uniquely determine such a script or class of coextensive scripts. Given a performance, the dialogue can be univocally transcribed: different correct ways of writing it down will have exactly the same performances as compliants. But this is not true of the rest of the text. A given setting, for example, may comply with extensionally divergent descriptions; and its compliance with some descriptions may be theoretically undecidable. The parts of the text other than the dialogue count not as integral parts of the defining score but as supplementary instructions. In the case of a novel consisting partly or even entirely of dialogue, the text is the work; but the same text taken as the text for a play is or contains the score for a work. The script for a silent film is neither the cinematic work nor a score for it but, though used in producing the film, is otherwise as loosely related to the work as is a verbal description of a painting to the painting itself.

8. Dance

The possibility of a notation for the dance was one of the initial questions that led to our study of notational systems. Because the dance is visual like painting, which has no notation, and yet transient and temporal like music, which has a highly developed standard notation, the answer is not altogether obvious; and ill-grounded negatives and irresponsible affirmatives have been put forth about equally often.

The ill-grounded negatives rest on the argument that the dance, as a visual and mobile art involving the infinitely subtle and varied expressions and three-dimensional motions of one or more highly complex organisms, is far too complicated to be captured by any notation. But, of course, a score need not capture all the subtlety and complexity of a performance. That would be hopeless even in the comparatively simpler art of music, and would always be pointless. The function of a score is to specify the essential properties a performance must have to belong to the work; the stipulations are only of certain aspects and only within certain degrees. All other variations are permitted; and the differences among performances of the same work, even in music, are enormous.

The irresponsible affirmative answers consist of pointing out that a notation can be devised for almost anything. This, of course, is irrelevant. The significant issue is whether in terms of notational language we can provide real definitions that will identify a dance in its several performances, independently of any particular history of production.

For such real definitions to be possible there must, as we have seen, be an antecedent classification of performances into works that is similarly independent of history of production. This classification need not be neat or complete but must serve as a foil, a scaffolding, a springboard, for the development of a full and systematic classification.

That the requisite antecedent classification exists for the dance seems clear. Prior to any notation, we make reasonably consistent judgments as to whether performances by different people are instances of the same dance. No theoretical barrier stands in the way of developing a suitable notational system.

Practical feasibility is another matter, not directly in question here. The antecedent classification is so rough and tentative that the decisions to be made are many, intricate, and consequential. And inadvertent violation of one of the syntactic or semantic requirements can easily result in a non-notational language or a system that is no language at all. Bold and intelligent systematization is called for, along with a good deal of care.

Among notations that have been proposed for the dance, the one called *Labanotation* [21] after the inventor, Rudolf Laban, seems deservedly to have gained most recognition. An impressive scheme of analysis and description, it refutes the common belief that continuous complex motion

[21] Laban was working on the matter in Vienna as early as the 1920's. He published *Choreographie* (Jena, Eugen Diederichs, 1926); *Effort*, with F. C. Lawrence (London, MacDonald & Evans, Ltd., 1947); and *Principles of Dance and Movement Notation* (London, MacDonald & Evans, Ltd., 1956). A convenient and well-illustrated exposition by Ann Hutchinson is available in a paperback book, *Labanotation* (Norfolk, Conn., New Directions, 1961), which is cited in the next three footnotes. One of the competing systems has been proposed by Rudolf and Joan Benesh in *An Introduction to Dance Notation* (London, Adam & Charles Black, Ltd., 1956). I leave it as an exercise for the reader to compare the Laban and Benesh systems in the light of the principles set forth in the present book.

is too recalcitrant a subject-matter for notational articulation, and discredits the dogma that successful systematic description depends in general upon some inherent amenability—some native structural neatness—in what is described. Indeed, the development of Laban's language offers us an elaborate and intriguing example of the process that has come to be called "concept formation".

How far, though, does the system meet the theoretical requirements for a notational language? I can answer only tentatively, from an inadequate knowledge of the system. That the characters are syntactically disjoint seems clear. Satisfaction of the requirements of finite differentiation is less easily ascertained; but Laban avoids a good many pitfalls here. For example, one naturally looks for a violation in the directional indications, since if every different angle of a line stands for a different direction, neither the syntactic nor the semantic requirement of differentiation is fulfilled. But in Labanotation, direction of facing is indicated by a "direction pin" in any of eight positions disposed at equal intervals around the full horizontal circle (Figure 12);

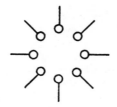

Figure 12

and a direction halfway between any two proximate directions among these eight is indicated by combining the signs for the two (e.g., as in Figure 13).

Figure 13

This device admits of no further iteration to indicate directions between two proximate directions among the sixteen. Elsewhere in the system, differentiation is often achieved just as decisively as here. One is alerted for trouble by such a statement as: "The relative length of the direction symbol shows its time value"; but here, as in music, time is divided into beats, and the least difference in duration provided for in the language is presumably the same as in standard musical notation.[22]

Like standard musical notation, Labanotation provides for more and less specific scoring, and so violates the condition of semantic disjointness. The *ad lib* signs and the explicit license to describe in detail or leave open certain

---

[22] Or less. The least duration indicated by any of the characters actually presented or mentioned in *Labanotation* (p. 52) is one-sixteenth of a beat, probably because at even the slowest normal tempo, that is the shortest time in which a dancer can be expected to execute a distinct and recognizable unit of movement. But so long as a limit is set, just where does not matter.

aspects of a movement [23] have much the same effect as do the free-cadenza and figured-bass notations in music. The result is that identity of a work will not be preserved in every chain of alternating steps between scores and performances. The flexibility offered may be welcomed by the choreographer or composer, and does not affect score-to-performance steps; but it leaves the performance-to-score steps insufficiently determined until the specificity of the scoring is stipulated. Labanotation as a whole is a discursive language comprising several notational subsystems; and in some cases, a class of performances may be a work relative to one but not another of these notational systems.

So far, I have been considering only the basic vocabulary. Some of the other symbolism introduced cannot be embraced in any notational system. A prime example is the use of words or pictures to indicate physical objects involved in the dance.[24] If object-words in general are ad-

[23] For use of the *ad lib* signs, see *Labanotation*, pp. 88, 187. On permitted variance in specificity of scoring, see e.g., pp. 59, 262. In such passages we find, I think, the significance of the introductory statement: "Labanotation allows for any degree of specificity" (p. 6). Read as meaning that the system allows for specification to within any given degree of precision whatsoever, this statement would imply lack of differentiation.

Incidentally, Labanotation seems to be redundant, although whether alternative symbols are actually coextensive is not always clear from the exposition (e.g., see p. 144). We have seen that coextensive characters in music sometimes differ in meaning through entering into parallel compounds that differ in extension; so far I have not discovered any analogue of this in Labanotation.

[24] *Labanotation*, pp. 179–181.

mitted, then semantic disjointness and differentiation are sacrificed and we have a discursive language. If object-sketches in general are admitted, then syntactic differentiation goes by the board, too, and we do not even have a language. One remedy would be to restrict the admitted words or pictures very severely in appropriate ways. Another, suggested earlier for tempo-words in music and stage directions in the drama, would be to treat these characters not as integral parts of a score at all but as supplementary and nondefinitive. Whether this is fitting depends upon whether (as seems fair enough) a performance employing different objects or even none is an instance of the same dance, just as a performance of *Hamlet* in modern dress and without scenery or accessories is an instance of the same play.

All in all, Labanotation passes the theoretical tests very well—about as well as does ordinary musical notation, and perhaps as well as is compatible with practicality. I am not saying that we have here a good or effective notational system for the dance, that the decisions embodied in it are sound or happy or consistent. Such an appraisal by a layman would be impertinent and worthless. By extensive use, the language may be found unsatisfactory or become traditional enough to acquire authority. If this or another language becomes standard enough, its underlying analysis of movement into factors and particles will prevail; arbitrary decisions will blossom into absolute truth, and expedient units for discourse ripen into the ultimate components of reality—awaiting revolution.

Laban conceived his system as a notation not merely for

dance but for human movement in general, and went on to develop and supplement the system as a means for analyzing and classifying all human physical activities. The need for some such system is especially apparent, for example, in industrial engineering and in psychological experimentation. Whether the experimenter or the subject repeats his behavior on a second occasion depends upon the criteria of identity of behavior that are applied; and the problem of formulating such criteria is the problem of developing a notational system. As for nonhuman movement, a zoologist has recently proposed an entertaining and illuminating method of codifying the various gaits of horses.[25]

9. Architecture

The architect's papers are a curious mixture. The specifications are written in ordinary discursive verbal and numerical language. The renderings made to convey the appearance of the finished building are sketches. But what of the plans?

Because a plan is a drawing, with lines and angles subject to continuous variation, the first guess would be that it is technically a sketch. But on the plan are measurements in words and figures. This suggests that we have here a combination of sketch and script. But I think this again is wrong. In the first place, the drawing is used only to indicate the relative location of elements and measurements.

[25] See Milton Hildebrand, "Symmetrical Gaits of Horses", *Science*, vol. 150 (1965), pp. 701–708.

Careful drawing to scale is merely for convenience and elegance; a rough and distorted version, with the same letters and numerals, qualifies as a true copy of the most precisely drafted blueprint, prescribes the constitutive properties as rigorously, and has the same buildings as compliants. In the second place, while the numerals as characters in the unlimited set of fractional numerals are scripts, the numerals admissible in architectural plans are tacitly restricted—e.g., so that measurements are to be given only, say, to the nearest thirty-second of an inch. So long as any such restriction is in force, the admitted part of numerical language does not, like the whole, violate the condition of finite differentiation, but qualifies as notational. Thus although a drawing often counts as a sketch, and a measurement in numerals as a script, the particular selection of drawing and numerals in an architectural plan counts as a digital diagram and as a score.

Architectural plans, like musical scores, may sometimes define works as broader than we usually take them. For the architect's specifications of materials and construction (whether written out separately or on the plans) can no more be considered integral parts of a score than can the composer's verbal specifications of tempo. An architect is free to stipulate that the material of a foundation be stone, or that it be granite, or that it be Rockport seam-faced granite. Given the building, we cannot tell which of these nesting terms occurs in the specifications. The class of buildings picked out by the plans-plus-specifications is narrower than that defined by the plans alone; but the plans-plus-specifications make up a script, not a score. Thus the question whether two buildings are instances of the same work, relative to the architect's total language, is an indeterminate one. Relative to the notational language of plans, it is determinate; but the work is then identified with a more comprehensive class than is customary. However, exact conformity between definition and ordinary practice is never required or to be expected.

We must not be misled by the fact that the compliance-class of a set of plans happens so often to consist of but one building; or by the preeminent interest or value that a given instance of an architectural work may have; or by the emphasis sometimes laid upon immediate supervision, by the architect, of the process of construction. Many a composition is played only once; certain performances of other pieces have exceptional importance; and a building or performance executed under the direction of the designer or composer, while a more personal product and perhaps much better (or much worse) than another building or performance from the same plans or score, is not therefore a more authentic or original instance of the work.

Nevertheless, the work of architecture is not always as surely disengaged from a particular building as is a work of music from a particular performance. The end-product of architecture, unlike that of music, is not ephemeral; and the notational language was developed in response rather to the need for participation of many hands in construction. The language thus has weaker warrant for, and meets more resistance in, overriding the primordial autographic stage of the art. Plainly enough, all houses complying with the plans for Smith-Jones Split-Level #17 are equally instances of that architectural work. But in the case of an earlier architectural tribute to womanhood, the Taj Mahal, we may bridle at considering another building from the same plans and even on the same site to be an instance of the same work rather than a copy. We are not as comfortable about identifying an architectural work with a design rather than a building as we are about identifying a musical work with a composition rather than a performance. In that architecture has a reasonably appropriate notational system and that some of its works are unmistakably allographic, the art is allographic. But insofar as its notational language has not yet acquired full authority to divorce identity of work in all cases from particular production, architecture is a mixed and transitional case.

In the present chapter I have been applying, chiefly to symbol systems in the arts, principles developed in Chapter IV in response to questions raised in Chapter III. The reader will already have discerned that these principles have some bearing upon problems left unresolved in the first two chapters. I now turn to those problems again and to other unfinished business.

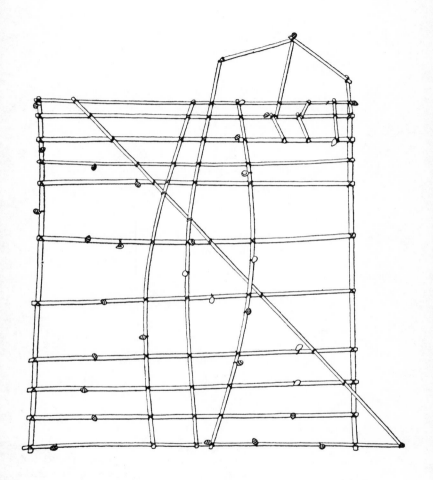

Reverse

Chart made by the Marshall Islanders. Seashells stand for
islands, bamboo strips for prevailing winds and currents.
Courtesy of the Peabody Museum, Harvard University.
Drawing by Symme Burstein.

VI

ART AND THE UNDERSTANDING

*Science . . . is willing to accept a theory that vastly out-
reaches its evidential basis if that theory promises to exhibit an underlying order, a system of deep and simple
systematic connections among what had previously been a
mass of disparate and multifarious facts.*

C. G. Hempel *

1. Pictures and Paragraphs

Our explorations have led us by an improbable route
back to a problem left open in the first chapter. We saw
there that representation is not imitation and cannot be
defined in any of the popular ways. And the characterization of representation as denotation dependent upon pictorial properties was too *ad hoc* to be accepted as final; it
gave no insight into the crucial features that distinguish
representation from other modes of denotation. But now
the analysis of symbol systems undertaken in response to
the very different problem of allographic art has provided
means for clarifying the nature of representation.

A notational system, we saw, satisfies five requirements.
A language, notational or not, satisfies at least the first

* "Recent Problems of Induction" in *Mind and Cosmos* (Pittsburgh,
University of Pittsburgh Press, 1966), p. 132.

two: the syntactic requirements of disjointness and differentiation. Ordinary languages usually violate the remaining, semantic, requirements. Nonlinguistic systems differ from languages, depiction from description, the representational from the verbal, paintings from poems, primarily through lack of differentiation—indeed through density (and consequent total absence of articulation)—in the symbol scheme. Nothing is intrinsically a representation; status as representation is relative to symbol system. A picture in one system may be a description in another; and whether a denoting symbol is representational depends not upon whether it resembles what it denotes but upon its own relationships to other symbols in a given scheme. A scheme is representational only insofar as it is dense; and a symbol is a representation only if it belongs to a scheme dense throughout or to a dense part of a partially dense scheme. Such a symbol may be a representation even if it denotes nothing at all.

Consider, for example, some pictures in the traditional Western system of representation: the first is of a man standing erect at a given distance; the second, to the same scale, is of a shorter man at the same distance. The second image will be shorter than the first. A third image in this series may be of intermediate height; a fourth, intermediate between the third and second; and so on. According to the representational system, any difference in height among these images constitutes a difference in height of man represented. Whether any actual men are represented does not matter; all that is in question here is how the several images classify into characters, of which the images are marks. And no matter how delicate our discriminations may be, the classification provides for each picture many characters such that we cannot possibly determine that the picture belongs to at most a given one of them. Syntactic differentiation is absent throughout. Furthermore, while I have for simplicity considered only one dimension in this example, every difference in every pictorial respect makes a difference under our familiar system of representation.

The pictures in our example could as well have been centaur-pictures, of course; and even where there are denotata they need not form a dense field of reference. But representational systems are normally semantically dense,[1] even though vacuously so where the field of reference is entirely null.

Moreover, so long as the scheme provides for a dense set of characters, we need not actually have any pictures or images that are difficult to discriminate in height. We still have syntactic density here even if there are only two actual images and they differ conspicuously in height. Indeed, with only a single image, any character it belongs to will lack syntactic differentiation from others provided for by the scheme.

Although representation thus depends upon a relation-

---

[1] Those that are not semantically dense may be considered abnormal representational systems; but in what follows, "representational system" will often mean "normal representational system". Semantic density requires only that a dense set of reference-classes *be provided for*, not that the field of reference be *actually* dense. Incidentally, we have seen earlier that density is not implied by absence of differentiation throughout.

ship among symbols rather than upon their relationship to denotata, it nevertheless depends upon their use as denotative symbols. A dense set of elements does not constitute a representational scheme unless at least ostensibly provided with denotata. The rule for correlating symbols with denotata may result in no assignment of any actual denotata to any symbol, so that the field of reference is null; but elements become representations only in conjunction with some such correlation actual or in principle.

The articulation that distinguishes descriptions from representations is not, I must insist, a matter of their internal structure. Some writers have held that a linguistic (or 'discursive') symbol differs from a representational (or 'presentational') symbol in that a description is uniquely resolvable into particles such as words or letters while a picture is an indivisible whole. Actually, an atomic character such as a one-letter word is still a description while a compound picture such as a group portrait is still a representation. The significant difference lies in the relation of a symbol to others in a denotative system.

Distinguishing representations from descriptions in this way results in classing our usual system of pictorial representation with the symbol systems of seismographs and ungraduated thermometers. Plainly, some further distinctions are wanted. We have already examined in detail the most important differences among syntactically articulate systems—especially that between discursive and notational languages—but not the differences among syntactically dense systems. In our brief look at diagrams, maps, and models, we deferred consideration of such questions as how a purely graphic diagram differs from a painter's sketch, a contour map from an aerial photograph, a ship model from a sculpture.

Compare a momentary electrocardiogram with a Hokusai drawing of Mt. Fujiyama. The black wiggly lines on white backgrounds may be exactly the same in the two cases. Yet the one is a diagram and the other a picture. What makes the difference? Obviously, some feature of the different schemes in which the two marks function as symbols. But, since both schemes are dense (and assumed disjoint), what feature? The answer does not lie in what is symbolized; mountains can be diagrammed and heartbeats pictured. The difference is syntactic: the constitutive aspects of the diagrammatic as compared with the pictorial character are expressly and narrowly restricted. The only relevant features of the diagram are the ordinate and abscissa of each of the points the center of the line passes through. The thickness of the line, its color and intensity, the absolute size of the diagram, etc., do not matter; whether a purported duplicate of the symbol belongs to the same character of the diagrammatic scheme depends not at all upon such features. For the sketch, this is not true. Any thickening or thinning of the line, its color, its contrast with the background, its size, even the qualities of the paper—none of these is ruled out, none can be ignored. Though the pictorial and diagrammatic schemes are alike in not being articulate, some features that are constitutive in the pictorial scheme are dismissed as contingent in the diagrammatic scheme; the symbols in the pictorial scheme are relatively *replete*.[2]

While there is an at least theoretically sharp line between dense and articulate schemes, among dense schemes the difference between the representational and the diagrammatic is a matter of *degree*. We cannot say that no aspects of a representational painting, for example, are contingent; for such properties as weighing ten pounds or being in transit from Boston to New York on a certain day hardly affect the status of the painting in its representational scheme. Rather, one dense scheme is more diagrammatic than a second if the character-constitutive aspects under the first are properly included among the character-constitutive aspects under the second. One among a familiar category of familiar graphic schemes may come to be regarded as purely representational if its constitutive aspects include those of all the other schemes; then the schemes that exclude as contingent some of the constitutive aspects of this representational scheme are regarded as diagrammatic. The representational norm will of course itself be diagrammatic, under our definition, relative to abnormal schemes having additional constitutive aspects.

This all adds up to open heresy. Descriptions are distinguished from depictions not through being more arbitrary but through belonging to articulate rather than to dense

---

[2] Repleteness is thus distinguished both from generality of a symbol and from unlimitedness of a scheme, and is indeed entirely independent both of what a symbol denotes and of the number of symbols in a scheme. For the opposite of repleteness, I use the term "attenuation".

schemes; and words are more conventional than pictures only if conventionality is construed in terms of differentiation rather than of artificiality. Nothing here depends upon the internal structure of a symbol; for what describes in some systems may depict in others. Resemblance disappears as a criterion of representation, and structural similarity as a requirement upon notational or any other languages. The often stressed distinction between iconic and other signs becomes transient and trivial; thus does heresy breed iconoclasm.

Yet so drastic a reformation was imperative. It allows for full relativity of representation and for representation by things other than pictures. Objects and events, visual and nonvisual, can be represented by either visual or nonvisual symbols. Pictures may function as representations within systems very different from the one we happen to consider normal; colors may stand for their complementaries or for sizes, perspective may be reversed or otherwise transformed, and so on. On the other hand, pictures when taken as mere markers in a tactical briefing or used as symbols in some other articulate scheme do not function as representations. As we saw earlier, among representational systems, 'naturalism' is a matter of habit but habituation does not carry us across the boundary between description and representation. No amount of familiarity turns a paragraph into a picture; and no degree of novelty makes a picture a paragraph. A simple graphic diagram and a full-blown portrait differ from each other in degree but contrast sharply with a description and even with a purely connective diagram.

Our analysis of types of symbol schemes and systems thus enables us to deal with some stubborn problems concerning representation and description. At the same time, it unearths some unexpected affinities between pictures and seismograms and pointer-positions on ungraduated dials on the one hand, and between pictographs and circuit plans and words on the other. Some old and vague boundaries are transgressed, some significant new alliances and alienations effected.

One quite incidental consequence concerns representation in music. Here no more than in painting does representation require imitation. But if a performance of a work defined by a standard score denotes at all, it still does not represent; for as a performance of such a work it belongs to an articulate set. The same sound-event, taken as belonging to a dense set of auditory symbols, may represent. Thus electronic music without any notation or language properly so-called may be representational, while music under standard notation, if denotative at all, is descriptive. This is a minor curiosity, especially since denotation plays so small a role in music.

2. Searching and Showing

The familiar full pictorial scheme comprises whatever we take as a picture, and may be enlarged to include sculptures and some natural objects. Some characters of the scheme represent actual entities, some represent fictively, and some are not representational at all. Among those that are representational, as well as among those that are not, many are expressive; a character of the scheme may be representational or expressive or both or neither.

Representation and description, as we have seen, are denotative while exemplification and expression run in the opposite direction from denotation. Since the pictorial characters remain the same in the representational and expressive systems, pictorial expression as well as pictorial representation is by symbols from a dense scheme; but density, although necessary for representation, is not (as the case of expressive language will show) necessary for expression. Ordinary realistic representation has been identified above as a particular familiar system within the species of dense and relatively replete denotational systems; but ordinary pictorial expression had already been identified earlier as the metaphorical portion of a particular familiar system within the species of exemplificational systems. While adequate general characterization of representation had to await introduction of the technical concepts discussed in Chapters IV and V, a comparable general characterization of expression had already been accomplished in other terms in Chapter II.

Expression and exemplification in the arts exhibit, nevertheless, a variety of combinations of syntactic and semantic features such as we used in classifying denotative systems. Of course, the semantic properties of ambiguity, disjointness, differentiation, density, and discontinuity must now be defined more generally, in terms of reference and reference-classes rather than of compliance (or denotation) and compliance-classes (or extensions); but the way of doing this is obvious. For example, a system is semantically differentiated in this broader sense if and only if for every two characters K and K' and every element h not referred to by both, determination either that K does not refer to h or that K' does not refer to h is theoretically possible. The narrower definitions were used earlier because we were concerned exclusively with denotative systems. Exemplificational systems, no matter what their syntactic and semantic properties, do not qualify as notations or languages.

In painting and sculpture, exemplification is syntactically and semantically dense. Neither the pictorial characters nor the exemplified properties are differentiated; and exemplified predicates come from a discursive and unlimited natural language. Comparison with the case of an ungraduated thermometer is pertinent here as in the case of representation; but now the pictures are to be compared rather with the temperature-occasions than with the mercury-column-heights. For the pictures, like the temperature-occasions, are rather denoted than denoting under the systems in question.

Pictorial exemplification, like representation, differs from the comparable symbol system of the thermometer in being much less narrowly confined. Pictures may exemplify colors, shapes, sounds, feelings, etc.; and the closer comparison would be with a versatile and complicated gauge, or a battery of them. Narrower systems of exemplification, confined say to the exemplification of colors, are to the full system somewhat as diagrammatic systems are to representation. But while attrition from the representational to the diagrammatic is by restriction upon the constitutive syntactic aspects of the symbols, attrition from full to narrower pictorial exemplification is by restriction upon the constitutive aspects of what is symbolized. The exemplifying symbols remain constant; any pictorial aspect of a picture may participate, for example, in exemplification of a color or expression of a sound. Thus these narrower systems of exemplification, unlike diagrammatic systems, remain pictorial in the sense that their symbols are no less replete than are those of the full systems of pictorial exemplification and representation.

If seeing what properties a picture exemplifies or expresses is like applying an ungraduated meter, *saying* what the picture exemplifies is a matter of fitting the right words from a syntactically unlimited and semantically dense language. However exact any term we apply, there is always another such that we cannot determine which of the two is actually exemplified by the picture in question. Since the language is also discursive, containing terms that extensionally include others, we can decrease the risk of error by using more general terms; but safety is then gained by sacrifice of precision. Compare the process of measuring an object. As noticed earlier, exactness is improved but our ability to establish correctness diminished as we carry our answer to more and more decimal places. Saying what a picture exemplifies is like measuring with no set tolerances.

Pictorial exemplification is thus in effect an inverted system of gauging or measuring [3]; and pictorial expression is a particular system of metaphorical exemplification. In any such system with a dense symbol scheme and a dense or unlimited set of reference-classes, the search for accurate adjustment between symbol and symbolized calls for maximal sensitivity, and is unending. Moreover, what a pictorial character exemplifies or expresses depends not only upon what properties it has but upon which of these it symbolizes—functions as a sample of; and this is often much less clear than in the case of a tailor's swatch. The pictorial systems of exemplification are not nearly so standardized as most of our practical systems of sampling or gauging or measuring. I am by no means claiming that the details of the pictorial systems are before us for easy discovery; and I have offered no aid in deciding whether a given picture exemplifies a given property, or expresses a given feeling, but only an analysis of the symbolic relations of pictorial exemplification and expression wherever they may obtain.

A performance of a musical work usually not only belongs to or complies with but also exemplifies the work or score. [4] And since the works and scores belong to a nota-

[3] That is, the symbolic relation of the gauge-position or the numerical measurement to what is gauged or measured is denotation, while the relation of exemplification runs in the opposite direction, back from what is gauged or measured to the position or numeral. What makes for confusion is that the *process* of finding what a picture exemplifies runs in the same direction as the *process* of gauging or measuring.

[4] Just as objects may be said indifferently to exemplify the color red

tional system, we have here—in contrast to anything in pictorial exemplification—exemplification of what is articulate, disjoint, and limited.

A musical performance also normally exemplifies and expresses much beside the work or score. A property may be said elliptically [5] to be exemplified by the work if exemplified by all performances of the work. But this will seldom happen, since exemplified properties not prescribed by the score are nonconstitutive and may vary freely from performance to performance without affecting the status of any performance as a genuine (even if reprehensible) instance of the work. That we may have a limp performance of a heroic work is all too evident. What, though, can be meant here by saying the work is heroic? If we answer that to say the work is heroic is to say elliptically that all its *proper* performances are, "proper" cannot mean merely "compliant with the score". The propriety in question is rather compliance with supplementary instructions, verbal or otherwise, either printed along with the score or tacitly given by tradition, word-of-mouth, etc. We have seen (V,2) that in neither case can these instructions be taken as integral parts of the score, for they belong to a syntactically unlimited and semantically dense system, not to a

---

or the name "red" of that color, so performances may be said indifferently to exemplify a work or the score that has as its extension, and thus names, the work.

[5] But only elliptically. We cannot say the work actually exemplifies whatever all its instances exemplify; for if all the instances exemplify the work or the property of being an instance of the work, still the work does not exemplify that property.

notational language. And since performances taken as sound-events rather than as instances of works are not fully differentiated, exemplification of whatever is not prescribed by the score is, like pictorial exemplification, a matter of inverted gauging or measuring. So also in dance and drama. In all these cases, despite the definition of works by scores, exemplification or expression of anything beyond the score by a performance is reference in a semantically dense system, and a matter of infinitely fine adjustment.

In written literature, although the feelings and other properties exemplified [6] and expressed likewise belong to a dense set, the exemplifying and expressing symbols are articulate. In determining what a poem expresses we have before us a syntactically differentiated symbol and we seek precisely the property or properties from a certain dense set that the symbol is denoted by and refers to. This contrasts with gauging or measuring; for what is gauged or measured is never articulate.

The properties exemplified by a passage can be and often are provided with names from the same vocabulary —say English—as the words comprised in the passage itself; and we may consider a passage or a poem, as we do a painting, to exemplify the names of properties it exemplifies. Literary exemplification of such predicates or descrip-

---

[6] I am of course speaking here of literary exemplification, not merely of exemplification by literature. Some poems, like some paintings, may exemplify the property of being unsalable; but the exemplification is no more literary in the one case than pictorial in the other.

tions thus relates vocabularies, or the same vocabulary functioning at different levels; and both the symbol scheme and the field of reference are articulate and unlimited. The nature of the correlation established here has one rather remarkable result. The system read downward from the denoting or exemplified terms to the denoted or exemplifying work is, of course, syntactically articulate but semantically dense. Accordingly one might expect that for the system read in the opposite direction, from the exemplifying passage or work to the exemplified terms, the syntactic and semantic characteristics will be interchanged. Actually this system, too, is syntactically articulate and semantically dense. To see how this can be, consider the following case. Let a consist of all English terms, β of the unlimited subset of English temperature-terms. The syntactic ordering of each of these vocabularies is alphabetically-based (see V, note 13) and is articulate. The terms of β taken as denoting terms of a according to warmth are, however, densely ordered. The denotative system running from β to a is thus syntactically articulate but semantically dense. But now the terms of a taken according to warmth as exemplifying the terms of β are also densely ordered; and the exemplificational system running from a to β is likewise syntactically articulate but semantically dense. So in literature we have two (perhaps identical) syntactically articulate vocabularies, the terms of each taking the terms of the other as referents, with both of the resultant systems—the one a system of denotation, the other of exemplification—being syntactically articulate and semantically dense.[7] Thus even though a literary work is articulate and may exemplify or express what is articulate, endless search is always required here as in other arts to determine precisely what is exemplified or expressed.

Were we to take oral readings of a literary work to be performances of a score, what has been said above concerning musical performances would apply. But we found (V,7) reasons against this interpretation and in favor of taking utterances and inscriptions rather as siblings. Obviously, different utterances and inscriptions of the same character may exemplify and express different properties; properties exemplified or expressed by all utterances and inscriptions of a work may be said elliptically to be expressed by the work, and so may such other properties as are exemplified or expressed by all occurrences that qualify by established criteria as 'proper' utterances and inscriptions of the work. Variation among utterances and inscriptions in

---

[7] Apparently every system that is, conversely, syntactically dense but semantically articulate will have many vacant characters or many with the same reference-class. But a system that is syntactically and semantically dense may nevertheless be such that the reference-classes considered apart from the system are differentiated and normally ordered discontinuously throughout. For one such case, let each character consist of the class of straight marks that, for some fully reduced Arabic fraction m/n, are m/n inches long. (A mark is not an inscription in this scheme unless its length in inches is a rational number.) The scheme is syntactically dense. Now let each character take as referent the whole number that the m/n in question is correlated with in a particular integral ordering of the rationals. Then even though the set of whole numbers, however ordered, is differentiated throughout, each character of this syntactically dense system has its own reference-class, and the system is semantically dense. The semantic density here results from the way the whole numbers are related in the system to the characters referring to them.

what is exemplified or expressed is parallel (as we have seen) to variation in denotation among instances of an ambiguous term or indicator-word.

All this technical analysis seems remote enough from aesthetic experience, but I think some conception of the nature of the aesthetic and of the arts begins to emerge.

3. Action and Attitude

A persistent tradition pictures the aesthetic attitude as passive contemplation of the immediately given, direct apprehension of what is presented, uncontaminated by any conceptualization, isolated from all the echoes of the past and all the threats and promises of the future, exempt from all enterprise. By purification rites of disengagement and disinterpretation we are to seek a pristine, unsullied vision of the world. I need hardly recount the philosophic faults and aesthetic absurdities of such a view until someone seriously goes so far as to maintain that the appropriate aesthetic attitude toward a poem amounts to gazing at the printed page without reading it.

I have held, on the contrary, that we have to read the painting as well as the poem, and that aesthetic experience is dynamic rather than static. It involves making delicate discriminations and discerning subtle relationships, identifying symbol systems and characters within these systems and what these characters denote and exemplify, interpreting works and reorganizing the world in terms of works and works in terms of the world. Much of our experience and many of our skills are brought to bear and may be transformed by the encounter. The aesthetic 'attitude' is restless, searching, testing—is less attitude than action: creation and re-creation.

What, though, distinguishes such aesthetic activity from other intelligent behavior such as perception, ordinary conduct, and scientific inquiry? One instant answer is that the aesthetic is directed to no practical end, is unconcerned with self-defense or conquest, with acquisition of necessities or luxuries, with prediction and control of nature. But if the aesthetic attitude disowns practical aims, still aimlessness is hardly enough. The aesthetic attitude is inquisitive as contrasted with the acquisitive and self-preservative, but not all nonpractical inquiry is aesthetic. To think of science as motivated ultimately by practical goals, as judged or justified by bridges and bombs and the control of nature, is to confuse science with technology. Science seeks knowledge without regard to practical consequences, and is concerned with prediction not as a guide for behavior but as a test of truth. Disinterested inquiry embraces both scientific and aesthetic experience.

Attempts are often made to distinguish the aesthetic in terms of immediate pleasure; but troubles arise and multiply here. Obviously, sheer quantity or intensity of pleasure cannot be the criterion. That a picture or poem provides more pleasure than does a proof is by no means clear; and some human activities unrelated to any of these provide enough more pleasure to render insignificant any differences in amount or degree among various types of inquiry. The claim that aesthetic pleasure is of a different and superior *quality* is by now too transparent a dodge to be taken seriously.

The inevitable next suggestion—that aesthetic experience is distinguished not by pleasure at all but by a special aesthetic emotion—can be dropped on the waste-pile of 'dormitive virtue' explanations.

This clears the way for the sophisticated theory that what counts is not pleasure yielded but pleasure 'objectified', pleasure read into the object as a property thereof. Apart from images of some grotesque process of transfusion, what can this mean? To consider the pleasure as possessed rather than occasioned by the object—to say in effect that the object is pleased—may amount to saying that the object expresses the pleasure. But since some aesthetic objects are sad—express sadness rather than pleasure—this comes nowhere near distinguishing in general between aesthetic and nonaesthetic objects or experience.

Some of these difficulties are diminished and others obscured if we speak of satisfaction rather than pleasure. "Satisfaction" is colorless enough to pass in contexts where "pleasure" is ludicrous, hazy enough to blur counterinstances, and flexible enough to tolerate convenient vacillation in interpretation. Thus we may hope to lessen the temptation to conjure up a special quality or kind of feeling or to indulge in mumbo-jumbo about objectification. Nevertheless, satisfaction pretty plainly fails to distinguish aesthetic from nonaesthetic objects and experiences. Not only does some scientific inquiry yield much satisfaction, but some aesthetic objects and experiences yield none. Music and our listening, pictures and our looking, do not fluctuate between aesthetic and nonaesthetic as the playing or painting varies from exalted to excruciating. Being aesthetic does not exclude being unsatisfactory or being aesthetically bad.

The distinguishing feature, some say, is not satisfaction secured but satisfaction sought: in science, satisfaction is a mere by-product of inquiry; in art, inquiry is a mere means for obtaining satisfaction. The difference is held to be neither in process performed nor in satisfaction enjoyed but in attitude maintained. On this view the scientific *aim* is knowledge, the aesthetic *aim* satisfaction.

But how cleanly can these aims be separated? Does the scholar seek knowledge or the satisfaction of knowing? Obtaining knowledge and satisfying curiosity are so much the same that trying to do either without trying to do the other surely demands a precarious poise. And anyone who does manage to seek the satisfaction without seeking the knowledge will pretty surely get neither, while on the other hand abstention from all anticipation of satisfaction is unlikely to stimulate research. One may indeed be so absorbed in working on a problem as never to think of the satisfaction to be had from solving it; or one may dwell so fondly on the delights of finding a solution as to take no steps toward arriving at one. But if the latter attitude is aesthetic, aesthetic understanding of anything is foredoomed. And I cannot see that these tenuous, ephemeral, and idiosyncratic states of mind mark any significant difference between the aesthetic and the scientific.

4. The Function of Feeling

All these failures to arrive at an acceptable formulation
in terms of pleasure or satisfaction, yielded or 'objectified'
or anticipated, will hardly dislodge the conviction that the
distinction between the scientific and the aesthetic is somehow rooted in the difference between knowing and feeling, between the cognitive and the emotive. This latter
deeply entrenched dichotomy is in itself dubious on many
grounds, and its application here becomes especially puzzling when aesthetic and scientific experience alike are
seen to be fundamentally cognitive in character. But we
do not easily part with the idea that art is in some way or
other more emotive than is science.

The shift from pleasure or satisfaction to emotion-in-
general softens some of the crudities of the hedonistic
formulas but leaves us with trouble enough. Paintings and
concerts, and the viewing and hearing of them, need not
arouse emotion, any more than they need give satisfaction,
to be aesthetic; and anticipated emotion is no better criterion than anticipated satisfaction. If the aesthetic is charac-
teristically emotive in some way, we have yet to say in
what way.

Any picture of aesthetic experience as a sort of emotional bath or orgy is plainly preposterous. The emotions
involved tend to be muted and oblique as compared, for
example, with the fear or sorrow or depression or exulta-
tion that arises from actual battle or bereavement or defeat
or victory, and are not in general keener than the excitement or despair or elation that accompanies scientific ex-

ploration and discovery. What the inert spectator feels falls far short of what the characters portrayed on the stage feel, and even of what he himself would feel on witnessing real-life events. And if he leaps on the stage to participate, his response can no longer be called aesthetic. That art is concerned with simulated emotions suggests, as does the copy theory of representation, that art is a poor substitute for reality: that art is imitation, and aesthetic experience a pacifier that only partly compensates for lack of direct acquaintance and contact with the Real.

Often the emotions involved in aesthetic experience are not only somewhat tempered but also reversed in polarity. We welcome some works that arouse emotions we normally shun. Negative emotions of fear, hatred, disgust may become positive when occasioned by a play or painting. The problem of tragedy and the paradox of ugliness are made to order for ancient and modern Freudians, and the opportunity has not been neglected. Tragedy is said to have the effect of purging us of pent-up and hidden negative emotions, or of administering measured doses of the killed virus to prevent or mitigate the ravages of an actual attack. Art becomes not only palliative but therapeutic, providing both a substitute for good reality and a safeguard against bad reality. Theatres and museums function as adjuncts to Departments of Public Health.

Again, even among works of art and aesthetic experiences of evident excellence, the emotive component varies widely—from, say, a late Rembrandt to a late Mondrian, or from a Brahms to a Webern quartet. The Mondrian and the Webern are not obviously more emotive than Newton's or Einstein's laws; and a line between emotive and cognitive is less likely to mark off the aesthetic neatly from the scientific than to mark off some aesthetic objects and experiences from others.

All these troubles revive the temptation to posit a special aesthetic emotion or feeling or a special coloration of other emotions occurring in aesthetic experience. This special emotion or coloring may be intense when other emotions are feeble, may be positive when they are negative, and may occur in experience of the most intellectual art and yet be lacking in the most stirring scientific study. All difficulties are resolved—by begging the question. No doubt aesthetic emotions have the property that makes them aesthetic. No doubt things that burn are combustible. The theory of aesthetic phlogiston explains everything and nothing.

Thus two stubborn problems still confront us. First, despite our conviction that aesthetic experience is *some*how emotive rather than cognitive, the failure of formulae in terms of either yielded or anticipated emotions has left us with no way of saying *how*. Second, despite our recognition that emotion in aesthetic experience tends to be denatured and often even inverted, the obvious futility of explanations in terms of a special secretion of the aesthetic glands leaves us without any way of saying *why*. Perhaps the answer to the second question will be found in the answer to the first; perhaps emotion in aesthetic experience behaves as it does because of the role it plays.

Most of the troubles that have been plaguing us can, I have suggested, be blamed on the domineering dichotomy between the cognitive and the emotive. On the one side, we put sensation, perception, inference, conjecture, all nerveless inspection and investigation, fact, and truth; on the other, pleasure, pain, interest, satisfaction, disappointment, all brainless affective response, liking, and loathing. This pretty effectively keeps us from seeing that in aesthetic experience the *emotions function cognitively*. The work of art is apprehended through the feelings as well as through the senses. Emotional numbness disables here as definitely if not as completely as blindness or deafness. Nor are the feelings used exclusively for exploring the emotional content of a work. To some extent, we may feel how a painting looks as we may see how it feels. The actor or dancer—or the spectator—sometimes notes and remembers the feeling of a movement rather than its pattern, insofar as the two can be distinguished at all. Emotion in aesthetic experience is a means of discerning what properties a work has and expresses.

To say this is to invite hot denunciation for cold over-intellectualization; but rather than aesthetic experience being here deprived of emotions, the understanding is being endowed with them. The fact that emotions participate in cognition no more implies that they are not felt than the fact that vision helps us discover properties of objects implies that color-sensations do not occur. Indeed, emotions must be felt—that is, must occur, as sensations must—if they are to be used cognitively. Cognitive use involves discriminating and relating them in order to gauge and grasp the work and integrate it with the rest of our experience and the world. If this is the opposite of passive absorption in sensations and emotions, it by no means amounts to canceling them. Yet it explains the modifications that emotions may undergo in aesthetic experience.

In the first place, a context of inquiry rather than of indulgence or incitement may result in a characteristic displacement of emotion. The psychological, physiological, and physical setting is different. A dollar earned, a dollar saved, a dollar spent, is still a dollar; affection eventuating in servitude, in frustration, in illumination, is still affection; but in neither case are all three quite the same. Emotions are not so self-contained as to be untouched by their environment, but cognitive use neither creates new emotions nor imparts to ordinary emotions some magic additive.

Furthermore, the frequent disparity between the emotion felt and the emotive content thereby discovered in the object is now readily understood. Pity on the stage may induce pity in the spectator; but greed may arouse disgust, and courage admiration. So may a white house look white at noon, but red at sunset; and a globe looks round from any angle.[8] Sensory and emotive experiences are related in complex ways to the properties of objects. Also, emotions function cognitively not as separate items but in combination with one another and with other means of knowing. Perception, conception, and feeling intermingle and interact; and an alloy often resists analysis into emotive and nonemotive components. The same pain (or is it the same?) tells of ice or fire. Are anger and indignation different feelings or the same feeling under different

[8] See SA, pp. 130–132.

circumstances? And does awareness of the overall difference arise from or lead to awareness of the difference in circumstances? The answers do not matter here; for I am not resting anything on the distinction between emotion and other elements in knowing, but rather insisting that emotion belongs with them. What does matter is that the comparisons, contrasts, and organization involved in the cognitive process often affect the participating emotions. Some may be intensified, as colors are against a complementary ground, or pointed up by subtle rhyming; others may be softened, as are sounds in a louder context. And some emotions may emerge as properties of the orchestrated whole, belonging like the shape of an eggshell to none of the lesser parts.

Again, negative emotions obviously function cognitively quite as well as positive ones. The horror and revulsion we may feel at *Macbeth* are not lesser means of understanding than the amusement and delight we may find in *Pygmalion*. We are not called upon to suppose that somehow—say by catharsis—the revulsion is transformed into delight, or to explain why the most forbidding portrait is as legitimately aesthetic as the most appealing one; for pleasantness in an emotion is no more a condition for cognitive functioning than is redness in a color-sensation. In aesthetic experience, emotion positive or negative is a mode of sensitivity to a work. The problem of tragedy and the paradox of ugliness evaporate.

Equally plainly, quantity or intensity of emotion is no measure of its cognitive efficacy. A faint emotion may be as informative as an overwhelming one; and finding that a work expresses little or no emotion can be as significant aesthetically as finding that it expresses much. This is something all attempts to distinguish the aesthetic in terms of amount or degree of emotion overlook.

Although many puzzles are thus resolved and the role of emotion in aesthetic experience clarified, we are still left without a way of distinguishing aesthetic from all other experience. Cognitive employment of the emotions is neither present in every aesthetic nor absent from every nonaesthetic experience. We have already noted that some works of art have little or no emotive content, and that even where the emotive content is appreciable, it may sometimes be apprehended by nonemotive means. In daily life, classification of things by feeling is often more vital than classification by other properties: we are likely to be better off if we are skilled in fearing, wanting, braving, or distrusting the right things, animate or inanimate, than if we perceive only their shapes, sizes, weights, etc. And the importance of discernment by feeling does not vanish when the motivation becomes theoretic rather than practical. The zoologist, psychologist, sociologist, even when his aims are purely theoretic, legitimately employs emotion in his investigations. Indeed, in any science, while the requisite objectivity forbids wishful thinking, prejudicial reading of evidence, rejection of unwanted results, avoidance of ominous lines of inquiry, it does not forbid use of feeling in exploration and discovery, the impetus of inspiration and curiosity, or the cues given by excitement over intriguing problems and promising hypotheses. And the more we discuss these matters, the more we come to realize that emotions are not so clearly differentiated or so sharply separable from other elements in cognition that the distinction can provide a firm basis for answering any moot questions.

5. Symptoms of the Aesthetic

Repeated failure to find a neat formula for sorting experiences into aesthetic and nonaesthetic, in rough conformity with rough usage, suggests the need for a less simpleminded approach. Perhaps we should begin by examining the aesthetic relevance of the major characteristics of the several symbol processes involved in experience, and look for aspects or symptoms, rather than for a crisp criterion, of the aesthetic. A symptom is neither a necessary nor a sufficient condition for, but merely tends in conjunction with other such symptoms to be present in, aesthetic experience.

Three symptoms of the aesthetic may be syntactic density, semantic density, and syntactic repleteness. As we have seen, syntactic density is characteristic of nonlinguistic systems, and is one feature distinguishing sketches from scores and scripts; semantic density is characteristic of representation, description, and expression in the arts, and is one feature differentiating sketches and scripts from scores; and relative syntactic repleteness distinguishes the more representational among semantically dense systems from the more diagrammatic, the less from the more 'schematic'. All three features call for maximum sensitivity of discrimination. Syntactic and semantic density demand endless attention to determining character and referent, given any mark of the system; and relative syntactic repleteness in a syntactically dense system demands such effort at discrimination along, so to speak, more dimensions. Impossiblity of finite determination may carry some suggestion of the ineffability so often claimed for, or charged against, the aesthetic. But density, far from being mysterious and vague, is explicitly defined; and it arises out of, and sustains, the unsatisfiable demand for absolute precision.

The fourth and final symptom of the aesthetic is the feature that distinguishes exemplificational from denotational systems and that combines with density to distinguish showing from saying. An experience is exemplificational insofar as concerned with properties exemplified or expressed—i.e., properties possessed and shown forth—by a symbol, not merely things the symbol denotes. Counting such exemplificationality as aesthetic may seem a concession to the tradition that associates the aesthetic with the immediate and nontransparent and so insists that the aesthetic object be taken for what it is in itself rather than as signifying anything else. But exemplification, like denotation, relates a symbol to a referent, and the distance from a symbol to what applies to or is exemplified by it is no less than the distance to what it applies to or denotes. As 'ineffability' upon analysis turns into density rather than mystery, 'immediacy' becomes a matter of exemplification rather than of intimacy—a function of direction rather than of distance. Nothing here implies that representation, in contrast with exemplification, is nonaesthetic. Exemplification contrasts with denotation rather than with representation. We saw that fictive representation and also representation-as are matters of exemplification; and representation in the arts is seldom explicitly factual and otherwise purely denotational. Moreover, an aesthetic experience need not exhibit all four symptoms.

The four symptoms probably tend to be present rather than absent, and to be prominent in aesthetic experience; but any of them may be absent from aesthetic or present in nonaesthetic experience. The symbolic vehicle of the literary arts, for example, is not syntactically dense, while the gauging of weights or temperatures may be dense both syntactically and semantically. Absence of some aesthetic or presence of some nonaesthetic symptom does not make for an aesthetically less pure totality, nor is an experience the more aesthetic the higher the concentration of aesthetic symptoms. Yet if the four symptoms listed are *severally* neither sufficient nor necessary for aesthetic experience, they may be *conjunctively* sufficient and *disjunctively* necessary; perhaps, that is, an experience is aesthetic if it has all these attributes and only if it has at least one of them.

I am not claiming that this proposal conforms faithfully to ordinary usage. Presystematic usage of "aesthetic" and "nonaesthetic" is even less clearly established by practice, and more seriously infected with inept theorizing, than in the case of most terms. I am rather suggesting that we have here an appropriate use for some badly abused terms. Density, repleteness, and exemplificationality, then, are earmarks of the aesthetic; articulateness, attenuation, and denotationality, earmarks of the nonaesthetic. A vague and yet harsh dichotomy of experiences gives way to a sorting of features, elements, and processes. Classification of a totality as aesthetic or nonaesthetic counts for less than identification of its aesthetic and nonaesthetic aspects. Phases of a decidedly aesthetic compound may be utterly nonaesthetic; for example, a score and its mere reading are devoid of all aesthetic aspects. On the other hand, aesthetic features may predominate in the delicate qualitative and quantitative discrimination required in testing some scientific hypotheses. Art and science are not altogether alien.

The distinction here drawn between the aesthetic and the nonaesthetic is independent of all considerations of aesthetic value. That is as it should be. An abominable performance of the *London Symphony* is as aesthetic as a superb one; and Piero's *Risen Christ* is no more aesthetic but only better than a hack's. The symptoms of the aesthetic are not marks of merit; and a characterization of the aesthetic neither requires nor provides a definition of aesthetic excellence.

6. The Question of Merit

Folklore has it that the good picture is pretty. At the next higher level, "pretty" is replaced by "beautiful", since the best pictures are often obviously not pretty. But again, many of them are in the most obvious sense ugly. If the beautiful excludes the ugly, beauty is no measure of aesthetic merit; but if the beautiful may be ugly, then "beauty" becomes only an alternative and misleading word for aesthetic merit.

Little more light is shed by the dictum that while science is judged by its truth, art is judged by the satisfaction it gives. Many of the objections urged earlier against satisfaction, yielded or anticipated, as a distinguishing feature of the aesthetic weigh also against satisfaction as a criterion of aesthetic merit: satisfaction cannot be identified with pleasure, and positing a special aesthetic feeling begs the question. We are left with the unhelpful formula that what is aesthetically good is aesthetically satisfactory. The question is what makes a work good or satisfactory.

Being satisfactory is in general relative to function and purpose. A good furnace heats the house to the required temperature evenly, economically, quietly, and safely. A good scientific theory accounts for the relevant facts clearly and simply. We have seen that works of art or their instances perform one or more among certain referential functions: representation, description, exemplification, expression. The question what constitutes effective symbolization of any of these kinds raises in turn the question what purpose such symbolization serves.

An answer sometimes given is that exercise of the symbolizing faculties beyond immediate need has the more remote practical purpose of developing our abilities and techniques to cope with future contingencies. Aesthetic experience becomes a gymnasium workout, pictures and symphonies the barbells and punching bags we use in strengthening our intellectual muscles. Art equips us for survival, conquest, and gain. And it channels surplus energy away from destructive outlets. It makes the scientist more acute, the merchant more astute, and clears the streets of juvenile delinquents. Art, long derided as the idle amusement of the guiltily leisure class, is acclaimed as a universal servant of mankind. This is a comforting view for those who must reconcile aesthetic inclinations with a conviction that all value reduces to practical utility.

More lighthearted and perhaps more simpleminded is the almost opposite answer: that symbolization is an irrepressible propensity of man, that he goes on symbolizing beyond immediate necessity just for the joy of it or because he cannot stop. In aesthetic experience, he is a puppy cavorting or a well-digger who digs doggedly on after finding enough water. Art is not practical but playful or compulsive. Dogs bark because they are canine, men symbolize because they are human; and dogs go on barking and men go on symbolizing when there is no practical need just because they cannot stop and because it is such fun.

A third answer, bypassing the issue over practicality versus fun, points to communication as the purpose of symbolizing. Man is a social animal, communication is a requisite for social intercourse, and symbols are media of communication. Works of art are messages conveying facts, thoughts, and feelings; and their study belongs to the omnivorous new growth called 'communications theory'. Art depends upon and helps sustain society—exists because, and helps ensure, that no man is an island.

Each of these explanations—in terms of gymnastics, play, or conversation—distends and distorts a partial truth. Exercise of the symbolizing skills *may* somewhat improve practical proficiency; the cryptographic character of symbol invention and interpretation *does* give them the fascination of a game; and symbols *are* indispensable to communication. But the lawyer or admiral improving his professional competence by hours in museums, the cavorting puppy, the neurotic well-digger, and the woman on the telephone do not, separately or together, give the whole picture. What all three miss is that the drive is curiosity and the aim enlightenment. Use of symbols beyond immediate need is for the sake of understanding, not practice; what compels is the urge to know, what delights is discovery, and communication is secondary to the apprehension and formulation of what is to be communicated. The primary purpose is cognition in and for itself; the practicality, pleasure, compulsion, and communicative utility all depend upon this.

Symbolization, then, is to be judged fundamentally by how well it serves the cognitive purpose: by the delicacy of its discriminations and the aptness of its allusions; by the way it works in grasping, exploring, and informing the world; by how it analyzes, sorts, orders, and organizes; by how it participates in the making, manipulation, retention, and transformation of knowledge. Considerations of simplicity and subtlety, power and precision, scope and selectivity, familiarity and freshness, are all relevant and often contend with one another; their weighting is relative to our interests, our information, and our inquiry.

So much for the cognitive efficacy of symbolization in general, but what of aesthetic excellence in particular? Distinguishing between the aesthetic and the meritorious cuts both ways. If excellence is not required of the aesthetic, neither is the excellence appropriate to aesthetic objects confined to them. Rather, the general excellence just sketched becomes aesthetic when exhibited by aesthetic objects; that is, aesthetic merit is such excellence in any symbolic functioning that, by its particular constellation of attributes, qualifies as aesthetic. This subsumption of aesthetic under cognitive excellence calls for one more reminder that the cognitive, while contrasted with both the practical and the passive, does not exclude the sensory or the emotive, that what we know through art is felt in our bones and nerves and muscles as well as grasped by our minds, that all the sensitivity and responsiveness of the organism participates in the invention and interpretation of symbols.

The problem of ugliness dissolves; for pleasure and prettiness neither define nor measure either the aesthetic experience or the work of art. The pleasantness or unpleasantness of a symbol does not determine its general cognitive efficacy or its specifically aesthetic merit. *Macbeth* and the Goya *Witches' Sabbath* no more call for apology than do *Pygmalion* and the Botticelli *Venus*.

The dynamics of taste, often embarrassing to those who seek inflexible standards of immutable excellence, also become readily understandable. After a time and for a time, the finest painting may pall and the greatest music madden. A work may be successively offensive, fascinating, comfortable, and boring. These are the vicissitudes of the vehicles and instruments of knowledge. We focus upon frontiers; the peak of interest in a symbol tends to occur at the time of revelation, somewhere midway in the passage from the obscure to the obvious. But there is endurance and renewal, too. Discoveries become available knowledge only when preserved in accessible form; the trenchant and laden symbol does not become worthless when it becomes familiar, but is incorporated in the base for further exploration. And where there is density in the symbol system, familiarity is never complete and final; another look may always disclose significant new subtleties. Moreover, what we read from and learn through a symbol varies with what we bring to it. Not only do we discover the world through our symbols but we understand and reappraise our symbols progressively in the light of our growing experience. Both the dynamics and the durability of aesthetic value are natural consequences of its cognitive character.

Like considerations explain the relevance to aesthetic merit of experience remote from the work. What a Manet or Monet or Cézanne does to our subsequent seeing of the world is as pertinent to their appraisal as is any direct confrontation. How our lookings at pictures and our listenings to music [9] inform what we encounter later and elsewhere is integral to them as cognitive. The absurd and awkward myth of the insularity of aesthetic experience can be scrapped.

The role of theme and variation—common in architecture and other arts as well as in music—also becomes intel-

[9] Music can inform perception not only of other sounds but also of the rhythms and patterns of what we see. Such cross-transference of structural properties seems to me a basic and important aspect of learning, not merely a matter for novel experimentation by composers, dancers, and painters.

ligible. Establishment and modification of motifs, abstraction and elaboration of patterns, differentiation and interrelation of modes of transformation, all are processes of constructive search; and the measures applicable are not those of passive enjoyment but those of cognitive efficacy: delicacy of discrimination, power of integration, and justice of proportion between recognition and discovery. Indeed, one typical way of advancing knowledge is by progressive variation upon a theme. Among modern composers, theme and variation along with all recognizable pattern is sometimes scorned, and maximum unpredictability is the declared aim; but, as C. I. Lewis pointed out,[10] complete irregularity is inconceivable—if no sequence is ever repeated in a given composition, that fact in itself constitutes a notable regularity.

Aesthetic merit, however, has by no means been my main concern in this book, and I am somewhat uncomfortable about having arrived at an incipient definition of what is often confusingly called 'beauty'. Excessive concentration on the question of excellence has been responsible, I think, for constriction and distortion of aesthetic inquiry.[11] To say that a work of art is good or even to say how good it is does not after all provide much information, does not tell us whether the work is evocative, robust, vibrant, or exquisitely designed, and still less what are its salient specific qualities of color, shape, or sound. More-

[10] *Mind and the World Order* (New York, Charles Scribner's Sons, 1929), p. 385.

[11] Cf. my "Merit as Means" in *Art and Philosophy*, ed. S. Hook (New York, New York University Press, 1966), pp. 56–57.

over, works of art are not race-horses, and picking a winner is not the primary goal. Rather than judgments of particular characteristics being mere means toward an ultimate appraisal, judgments of aesthetic value are often means toward discovering such characteristics. If a connoisseur tells me that one of two Cycladic idols that seem to me almost indistinguishable is much finer than the other, this inspires me to look for and may help me find the significant differences between the two. Estimates of excellence are among the minor aids to insight. Judging the excellence of works of art or the goodness of people is not the best way of understanding them. And a criterion of aesthetic merit is no more the major aim of aesthetics than a criterion of virtue is the major aim of psychology.

In short, conceiving of aesthetic experience as a form of understanding results both in resolving and in devaluing the question of aesthetic value.

7. Art and the Understanding

In saying that aesthetic experience is cognitive experience distinguished by the dominance of certain symbolic characteristics and judged by standards of cognitive efficacy, have I overlooked the sharpest contrast: that in science, unlike art, the ultimate test is truth? Do not the two domains differ most drastically in that truth means all for the one, nothing for the other?

Despite rife doctrine, truth by itself matters very little in science. We can generate volumes of dependable truths at will so long as we are unconcerned with their importance; the multiplication tables are inexhaustible, and empirical truths abound. Scientific hypotheses, however true, are worthless unless they meet minimal demands of scope or specificity imposed by our inquiry, unless they effect some telling analysis or synthesis, unless they raise or answer significant questions. Truth is not enough; it is at most a necessary condition. But even this concedes too much; the noblest scientific laws are seldom quite true. Minor discrepancies are overridden in the interest of breadth or power or simplicity.[12] Science denies its data as the statesman denies his constituents—within the limits of prudence.

Yet neither is truth one among competing criteria involved in the rating of scientific hypotheses. Given any assemblage of evidence, countless alternative hypotheses conform to it. We cannot choose among them on grounds of truth; for we have no direct access to their truth. Rather, we judge them by such features as their simplicity and strength. These criteria are not supplemental to truth but applied hopefully as a means for arriving at the nearest approximation to truth that is compatible with our other interests.

Does this leave us with the cardinal residual difference that truth—though not enough, not necessary, and not a touchstone for choosing among hypotheses—is nevertheless a consideration relevant in science but not in art? Even so meek a formulation suggests too strong a contrast.

[12] See my "Science and Simplicity" in *Philosophy of Science Today*, ed. S. Morgenbesser (New York, Basic Books, Inc., 1967), pp. 68–78.

Truth of a hypothesis after all is a matter of fit—fit with a body of theory, and fit of hypothesis and theory to the data at hand and the facts to be encountered. And as Philipp Frank liked to remind us, goodness of fit takes a two-way adjustment—of theory to facts and of facts to theory —with the double aim of comfort and a new look. But such fitness, such aptness in conforming to and reforming our knowledge and our world, is equally relevant for the aesthetic symbol. Truth and its aesthetic counterpart amount to appropriateness under different names. If we speak of hypotheses but not of works of art as true, that is because we reserve the terms "true" and "false" for symbols in sentential form. I do not say this difference is negligible, but it is specific rather than generic, a difference in field of application rather than in formula, and marks no schism between the scientific and the aesthetic.

None of this is directed toward obliterating the distinction between art and science. Declarations of indissoluble unity—whether of the sciences, the arts, the arts and sciences together, or of mankind—tend anyway to focus attention upon the differences. What I am stressing is that the affinities here are deeper, and the significant differentia other, than is often supposed. The difference between art and science is not that between feeling and fact, intuition and inference, delight and deliberation, synthesis and analysis, sensation and cerebration, concreteness and abstraction, passion and action, mediacy and immediacy, or truth and beauty, but rather a difference in domination of certain specific characteristics of symbols.

ART AND THE UNDERSTANDING

The implications of this reconception may go beyond philosophy. We hear a good deal about how the aptitudes and training needed for the arts and for the sciences contrast or even conflict with one another. Earnest and elaborate efforts to devise and test means of finding and fostering aesthetic abilities are always being initiated. But none of this talk or these trials can come to much without an adequate conceptual framework for designing crucial experiments and interpreting their results. Once the arts and sciences are seen to involve working with—inventing, applying, reading, transforming, manipulating—symbol systems that agree and differ in certain specific ways, we can perhaps undertake pointed psychological investigation of how the pertinent skills inhibit or enhance one another; and the outcome might well call for changes in educational technology. Our preliminary study suggests, for example, that some processes requisite for a science are less akin to each other than to some requisite for an art. But let us forego foregone conclusions. Firm and usable results are as far off as badly needed; and the time has come in this field for the false truism and the plangent platitude to give way to the elementary experiment and the hesitant hypothesis.

Whatever consequences might eventually be forthcoming for psychology or education would in any case count as by-products of the theoretical inquiry begun here. My aim has been to take some steps toward a systematic study of symbols and symbol systems and the ways they function in our perceptions and actions and arts and sciences, and thus in the creation and comprehension of our worlds.

SUBJECT INDEX

SUBJECT INDEX

SUBJECT INDEX

NAME INDEX

275

NAME INDEX

NAME INDEX

Sessions, Roger, 127, 190n.
Shapiro, Harold, v
Shapiro, Meyer, v, 11n.
Sheppard, Richard, 91n.
Soulages, Pierre, 93
Stroop, J. R., *facing* 45, 60n.
Sturgis, Katharine, v

Taylor, J. G., 15n.
Thomson, Sir George, 177
Tingle, Immanuel, 112, 112n.
Turbayne, C. M., 36n., 71n.
Turing, A. M., 165n.

Urmson, J. O., 27n.

Venable, Lucy, v
Vermeer, Jan, 99, 106n., 110–111

Webern, Anton, 246
Weiss, P., 131n.
White, Burton L., 62n.
White, John, 17n.
Woolf, Virginia, 3

Yates, Peter, 190n.

277